Dear Reader,

In 2004, I was diagnosed with an inner-ear disorder called Ménière's disease. Rather than medication or surgery, my doctor prescribed a low-sodium DASH diet as my course of treatment. The idea that a change in diet could cure my ills seemed inconceivable at that point, but I did as instructed. I eliminated salt from my diet and modified my sodium intake to less than 1,500 milligrams per day.

Within weeks, I began noticing a change in my symptoms, and within months, the dizziness, deafness, and constant tinnitus I'd been experiencing for almost a year had virtually disappeared. It was the most miraculous physical transformation I'd ever experienced: concrete proof of the power of diet.

Whatever has brought you to the DASH diet, I am here to tell you: It works. Just as overly salted and heavily processed foods have the ability to harm your body, you have the power to help it heal, meal by healthy meal.

The DASH diet is intended to be a healthy eating plan for life, something to embrace and enjoy. I'm honored to join you on your journey to health, and wish you every happiness in the future.

Christy Ellingsworth

Welcome to the Everything® Series!

These handy, accessible books give you all you need to tackle a difficult project, gain a new hobby, comprehend a fascinating topic, prepare for an exam, or even brush up on something you learned back in school but have since forgotten.

You can choose to read an Everything® book from cover to cover or just pick out the information you want from our four useful boxes: Questions, Facts, Alerts, and Essentials. We give you everything you need to know on the subject, but throw in a lot of fun stuff along the way too.

question	**fact**
Answers to common questions.	Important snippets of information.

alert	**essential**
Urgent warnings.	Quick handy tips.

We now have more than 600 Everything® books in print, spanning such wide-ranging categories as cooking, health, parenting, personal finance, wedding planning, word puzzles, and so much more. When you're done reading them all, you can finally say you know Everything®!

PUBLISHER Karen Cooper

MANAGING EDITOR Lisa Laing

COPY CHIEF Casey Ebert

PRODUCTION EDITOR Jo-Anne Duhamel

ACQUISITIONS EDITOR Lisa Laing

DEVELOPMENT EDITOR Lisa Laing

EVERYTHING® SERIES COVER DESIGNER Erin Alexander

THE
EVERYTHING®
EASY
DASH
DIET
COOKBOOK

CHRISTY ELLINGSWORTH AND
MURDOC KHALEGHI, MD

200 QUICK AND EASY RECIPES FOR
WEIGHT LOSS AND BETTER HEALTH

ADAMS MEDIA
NEW YORK   LONDON   TORONTO   SYDNEY   NEW DELHI

Dedication

To those who struggle with their health and want to be whole again, it's time.

Acknowledgments

For their love and support always, I thank my family. And to the Big Guy, although I may sometimes wonder out loud, I trust you know what you're doing.—CE

Adams Media
An Imprint of Simon & Schuster, Inc.
57 Littlefield Street
Avon, Massachusetts 02322

Copyright © 2021 by Simon & Schuster, Inc.

All rights reserved, including the right to reproduce this book or portions thereof in any form whatsoever. For information, address Adams Media Subsidiary Rights Department, 1230 Avenue of the Americas, New York, NY 10020.

An Everything® Series Book.
Everything® and everything.com® are registered trademarks of Simon & Schuster, Inc.

First Adams Media trade paperback edition
January 2021

ADAMS MEDIA and colophon are trademarks of Simon & Schuster.

For information about special discounts for bulk purchases, please contact Simon & Schuster Special Sales at 1-866-506-1949 or business@simonandschuster.com.

The Simon & Schuster Speakers Bureau can bring authors to your live event. For more information or to book an event contact the Simon & Schuster Speakers Bureau at 1-866-248-3049 or visit our website at www.simonspeakers.com.

Interior design by Colleen Cunningham
Photographs by James Stefiuk

Manufactured in the United States of America

10 9 8 7 6 5 4 3 2 1

Library of Congress Cataloging-in-Publication Data
Names: Ellingsworth, Christy, author. | Khaleghi, Murdoc, author.
Title: The everything® easy DASH diet cookbook / Christy Ellingsworth and Murdoc Khaleghi, MD.
Description: First Adams Media trade paperback edition. | Avon, Massachusetts: Adams Media, 2021. | Series: Everything®. | Includes index.
Identifiers: LCCN 2020034718 | ISBN 9781507215210 (pb) | ISBN 9781507215227 (ebook)
Subjects: LCSH: Reducing diets--Recipes. | Hypertension--Diet therapy--Recipes. | LCGFT: Cookbooks
Classification: LCC RM222.2 .E438 2021 | DDC 641.5/6311--dc23
LC record available at https://lccn.loc.gov/2020034718

ISBN 978-1-5072-1521-0
ISBN 978-1-5072-1522-7 (ebook)

Contains material adapted from the following title published by Adams Media, an Imprint of Simon & Schuster, Inc.: The Everything® DASH Diet Cookbook by Christy Ellingsworth and Murdoc Khaleghi, MD, copyright © 2012, ISBN 978-1-4405-4353-1.

Contents

You Have the Power to Change Your Life

The DASH diet, or the Dietary Approaches to Stop Hypertension, is not just a diet. Quite simply, the DASH diet can change your life. Imagine if there were a medication that could significantly reduce your risk for heart disease, a stroke, or cancer, with the only side effects being weight loss and improved energy. What would that be worth to you? Now imagine you could achieve such a dramatic change in your life without having to take any medications. You just have to eat, something you already do anyway. All you need to actively do is change some of the foods you eat.

You may then think the foods you have to change to would be very restrictive, like a lot of the diets out there. Again, the DASH diet is not just a diet; it's a way to change your life. The only way to permanently change your life is to do something you can do permanently. Therefore, the DASH diet was designed to be something that you could easily incorporate into your life. You do not need to shop at special grocery stores or go through some of the difficult transition periods of other diets; you just need to start adjusting your food patterns, one step at a time.

The basics of the diet are simple: Eat more fruits and vegetables, whole grains, and lean protein, and eat less saturated fats, salt, and sweets. The problem with leaving it at that is there are no actual guidelines as to how much of what you should eat. The DASH diet fixes that problem.

The DASH diet is not just an idea that someone came up with and hoped might work. It was scientifically developed based on many large studies at several prestigious government, university, and hospital-research institutions. Its benefits have been repeatedly confirmed, and new benefits are always being discovered. The DASH diet has been repeatedly shown to improve many cholesterol and inflammatory biomarkers that are associated with risks for various diseases. You can easily see the impact on your own biomarkers through a service such as WellnessFX, and see the actual effects the DASH diet has on your own body.

For all these reasons, the DASH diet has been repeatedly rated as the Best Diet Overall in the world by several organizations, including *US News & World Report*. Unlike many diets that become a fad only to disappear as quickly as they became popular, the DASH diet's popularity has lasted for many years and is notably growing.

The biggest challenge of the DASH diet is making the dietary transition. This book is your key to making that transition. In addition to giving you the guidelines for the amounts of various foods you should eat, we actually provide you the recipes so you can start right away with eating delicious foods that follow the DASH diet.

The knowledge and tools in this book can change your life. All you need to supply is the motivation. Because you are reading this book, you already have. Congratulations on taking that first essential step to making your life healthier.

—Murdoc Khaleghi, MD

Introduction

Whether you picked up this book out of simple curiosity or dire need, *The Everything® Easy DASH Diet Cookbook* is intended to make life on a low-sodium diet easy and pleasurable. For those new to the diet, DASH is an acronym for Dietary Approaches to Stop Hypertension. The DASH diet is a healthy, balanced eating plan low in sodium and rich in fruits, vegetables, whole grains, and low-fat dairy products. Meats, sweets, and nuts are all permitted, although added sugars and fats should be eaten in moderation.

A low-sodium DASH diet is often prescribed for those with serious medical conditions and has been shown to aid the body in healing by lowering blood pressure, reducing cholesterol, and promoting heart health and wellness in general. As with many sensible eating plans, it has the added bonus of promoting healthy weight loss and weight maintenance, and may also aid in the prevention of cancer, osteoporosis, and diabetes. In short, the DASH diet has the potential for helping millions of people live longer, healthier lives.

But in order to benefit, you must make the commitment! In practice, many fall short because of the impracticality of dietary goals. Modern lives are endlessly busy, and because of this, good eating often takes a backseat until a health crisis erupts. *The Everything® Easy DASH Diet Cookbook* was written with this in mind. With two hundred simple, inexpensive, and delicious recipes—all with around 30 minutes or less of cooking time—there's no excuse not to make yourself and your health a priority.

On the DASH diet, you will be enjoying many of the same foods you've always eaten: fresh fruits and vegetables, low-fat dairy products, whole grains, beans, meats, even desserts. You will not feel deprived! But you will need to adapt. Salt-free living isn't easy, but it's worth it because *you're worth it*! Freeing yourself from the burden of bad health is a challenge to be taken to heart (pun intended).

The first step to starting the DASH diet is simple: Stop using salt. From there you'll need to stock a low-sodium pantry, seeking out products specifically created for a salt-free, low-sodium audience. It helps to purchase a small food-counts book until you're familiar with the sodium content of most common foods. You may want to keep it in your purse or pocket and consult it while shopping or dining out.

The good news is you can either buy or make everything you will need to live normally on the DASH diet. And as a low-sodium diet becomes more mainstream, companies are increasingly answering demand by expanding product lines, making salt-free cooking even easier and more convenient.

Use the recipes and information contained within this book to spark your own imagination. Wherever you live, seek out stores and scour for products that meet low-sodium criteria (140 milligrams or less per serving). Engage with the world around you—visiting local farms and farmers' markets—to buy the freshest and best produce, preferably organic whenever possible. New dishes will inevitably grow out of each season, and by incorporating the freshest ingredients, you'll be giving your body the best you possibly can. Outside of diet alone, explore every avenue at your disposal for healthy living. Join a gym, take an exercise class, or just go outside and take a walk, daily if possible. Look forward to spending time taking care of yourself.

A low-sodium diet is something you must commit to. You can't slack off and expect to make inroads. It can be hard, but don't give up. Your body will thank you! On those days when you feel as though you're simply treading water, remind yourself: You're in the pool! Those above you on the bleachers can see your progress, even when you can't. You may struggle with fatigue, but with daily practice you're building endurance, and ultimately, success.

CHAPTER 1
The DASH Diet

The DASH diet has become one of the most popular dietary lifestyles today. When many people hear the word *diet*, they assume it is temporary. The DASH diet is not meant to be temporary, though; it is designed to be a permanent lifestyle to make you healthier!

What Does DASH Mean?

DASH stands for Dietary Approaches to Stop Hypertension. Although the diet was created with a focus on hypertension, during the last decade it has been found to affect much more. The DASH diet has been shown to lower blood pressure, improve cholesterol, decrease the risk of many types of cancer, and even decrease the chance of kidney stones!

Show Me the Evidence

Unlike many dietary plans, the DASH diet has been put through rigorous scientific testing. It has been studied by the National Institutes of Health, the premier governmental research organization, and at many prestigious universities and medical centers through multicenter trials. Although the DASH diet itself does not have strict controls, the studies enforced strict controls on what subjects were eating to ensure the reliability of the data. Ever since those initial studies, the DASH diet continues to be studied in terms of how it might affect other diseases. New benefits are constantly being discovered.

fact

The DASH diet was originally formed with the goal of improving hypertension through diet. Since its formation, it has been found to have many other health benefits, from decreasing the risk of cancer to reducing the risk of heart attack and stroke.

Between all these benefits and how the DASH diet is designed to maximize compliance and sustainability, it is no wonder that the DASH diet is often considered the most popular diet among physicians and health organizations. In fact, *US News & World Report* magazine has repeatedly ranked the DASH diet as the number one overall diet plan.

High Blood Pressure

Hypertension, or high blood pressure, was the initial focus of the diet because hypertension is known to be one of the largest killers in American society. In addition, it is considered a "silent" killer, because you do not feel the effects of high blood pressure for years until it actually causes a heart attack or stroke. These occur when plaques that build up in our arteries clog a blood vessel and do not allow blood and oxygen flow to our heart and brain, respectively. A heart attack can result in the heart not being able to pump blood to the rest of the body, and a stroke can result in your brain being unable to control your body. Ultimately, heart attacks and strokes are the leading causes of death in our society, and strokes are a major cause of paralysis in those who survive them. By reducing the formation of these plaques, you can reduce your risk of death and disability. To reduce these plaques, you need to understand what causes them and how your diet contributes to them.

Blood pressure is the pressure your blood exerts on the blood vessel, which is also the pressure used by your heart to push blood through your body. The higher your blood pressure, the more damage that occurs to your blood vessels, with these damaged areas forming plaques that can cause a heart attack and stroke. This damage builds up over many years, which again is why high blood pressure is known as a silent killer, doing its damage during the course of many years. In addition, the higher your blood pressure, the harder your heart has to work; therefore, the more predisposed it becomes to failing. By controlling high blood pressure before it affects your body, you can successfully reduce your risk for a heart attack or stroke. Even more fortunately, no matter how long you may have had high blood pressure, you can still reduce your risk by acting on it now. In other words, it is never too late to help yourself.

---

alert

High blood pressure is considered one of the leading causes of death in developed nations. Because people do not feel the effects of high blood pressure for years, it is often called a "silent" killer.

Blood pressure is measured in millimeters of mercury, or mmHg. There are actually two blood pressure measurements: the pressure exerted by your heart and blood when it is actively pumping, or the *systolic* blood pressure, and the pressure exerted when the heart is not actively pumping, or the *diastolic* blood

pressure. Blood pressure measurements are displayed by showing the systolic blood pressure over the diastolic blood pressure. People who have a blood pressure greater than 140/90 mmHg are considered *hypertensives*, or to have high blood pressure.

Does the Diet Work?

The DASH diet has consistently and repeatedly been shown to successfully reduce blood pressure. The general consensus is that people with normal blood pressure following the diet have a reduction of about 6 mmHg in their systolic blood pressure and 3 mmHg in their diastolic blood pressure. People with high blood pressure experience approximately twice this reduction in both systolic and diastolic blood pressures.

---

question

Is the DASH diet just another fad diet?

The DASH diet has been repeatedly studied by many prestigious institutions and has been consistently shown to have many significant benefits to health. These effects have now been known for years and are verified again and again.

This sort of reduction can significantly reduce cardiovascular risk and is comparable to many blood pressure medications. Unlike costly blood pressure medications with their many deleterious side effects, the only side effects of the diet are improvement in blood pressure, cholesterol, cancer risk, and weight.

Why Does It Work?

The DASH diet is a sustainable lifestyle because it does not impose many of the strict restrictions that exist with many other diets. Rather than strict control of food or content choices, such as the number of grams of fat, the DASH diet is primarily driven by guidelines to make smart food choices. This lack of severe restriction allows you to gradually transition to a DASH diet, and maintain that lifestyle once fully transitioned. Other diets often require a sudden change, and have such tight restrictions it is impossible to maintain the diet for a long period of time.

The goals of the DASH diet are to reduce your intake of substances that hurt your body, and substitute that intake with more healthful substances. For example, rather than consuming foods high in saturated fat, sodium, and sugars, you eat more foods low in fat and sodium and high in protein and complex carbohydrates. It also makes sure that you eat even these healthful foods in moderation and not in excess.

You Are What You Eat

To best understand how the DASH diet affects your body, all you need is a basic primer in digestive physiology. The body absorbs three substances in food: protein, carbohydrates, and fat. Protein is primarily used for muscle and other tissue generation, while carbohydrates and fat are primarily used for energy. The body uses carbohydrates initially for energy, and then when low on those easily usable carbohydrates, the body starts to break down fat for energy. In other words, carbohydrate intake initially gets stored as "fat." Often people consume more carbohydrates than their bodies can initially use. In that situation, the body produces a hormone called insulin, which stores the carbohydrates in your body, and some of those excess carbohydrates are converted to stored fat as well.

What Your Body Sees

Carbohydrates, protein, and fat all have a certain amount of energy, which is measured in calories. The average person typically uses a little more than 2,000 calories per day. Carbohydrates and protein each have 4 calories per gram, while fats have 9 calories per gram. In other words, fats have more than double the energy per gram than carbohydrates and protein. Therefore, ingesting more fats will quickly increase the number of calories you take in, and by consuming excess calories you increase the storage of fat. Although there are good types of fat, which will be discussed later, in general the more stored fat you have, the worse that fat is, and therefore you want to decrease the amount of fat that is stored. Another way to decrease the storage of fat is to increase your activity, which will increase your energy consumption above the 2,000-calorie average. So by increasing your activity, you will consume fewer excess calories, and therefore store less fat.

Carbohydrates

Carbohydrates are the primary fuel for the body and have gotten a bad rap lately. Carbohydrates often get consumed in excess, causing an increase in the release of a hormone called *insulin*, which stores the carbohydrates as fat. Insulin spikes also make you feel fatigued and promote *insulin resistance*, a precursor for diabetes. Therefore, carbohydrates can be bad when too much enters the bloodstream at once but can appropriately fuel the body when consumed in moderation and with a steady release into the bloodstream. *Complex carbohydrates*, or carbohydrates that are linked together, are broken down more steadily when digested than *simple carbohydrates*, the types of sugars found in sweets, which do not have these same linkages. Simple carbohydrates enter the bloodstream all at once, giving you a sudden boost of energy, or "sugar rush," which soon goes away. Like decreasing your weight, having a steady, moderate consumption of complex carbohydrates will improve your energy and offer many other health benefits.

Sodium

Sodium is the primary ingredient in the most common form of salt. When you eat salt, sodium gets absorbed into your bloodstream. This increases the concentration of sodium in your blood compared to other tissues in your body. By *osmosis*, or the tendency of fluid to follow particles in that fluid, fluid in tissues flows back into the bloodstream. The more fluid there is in your bloodstream, the greater the pressure that fluid exerts on your heart and blood vessels, or the higher your blood pressure. Putting it all together, ingesting more salt increases your blood pressure.

Fat and Cholesterol: The Good and the Bad

As mentioned previously, high blood pressure creates damage to your blood vessels, which causes the formation of plaques that can lead to heart disease and stroke. What further contributes to this damage is the buildup of cholesterol-filled clots in excessive amounts of fat and cholesterol. Interestingly, though, certain types of fat and cholesterol seem to actually decrease this plaque formation. If you were to get your cholesterol measured, it would be broken down into certain good types of cholesterol, the most common being high-density lipoprotein (HDL) cholesterol, and certain bad types of cholesterol, the most common being low-density lipoprotein (LDL) cholesterol.

essential

Not all fat is bad; fats are an essential part of a healthy diet. The goal is to eat a moderate amount of healthy or unsaturated fatty acids, especially omega-3s, and to avoid saturated and trans fat.

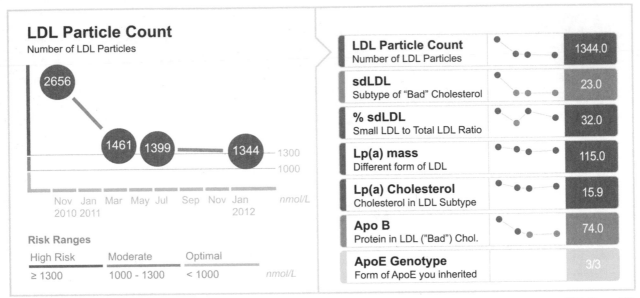

LDL Particle Count

Number of LDL Particles

2656

1461 1399 1344 1300
1000

Nov Jan Mar May Jul Sep Nov Jan   *nmol/L*
2010 2011   2012

Risk Ranges

High Risk	Moderate	Optimal
≥ 1300	1000 - 1300	< 1000

nmol/L

LDL Particle Count Number of LDL Particles		1344.0
sdLDL Subtype of "Bad" Cholesterol		23.0
% sdLDL Small LDL to Total LDL Ratio		32.0
Lp(a) mass Different form of LDL		115.0
Lp(a) Cholesterol Cholesterol in LDL Subtype		15.9
Apo B Protein in LDL ("Bad") Chol.		74.0
ApoE Genotype Form of ApoE you inherited		3/3

Printed with copyright permission courtesy of WellnessFX.

Generally, HDL cholesterol decreases plaque formation, and LDL cholesterol increases plaque formation. Actually, your physiology is far more complex than these two common lipoproteins, as they have many different subtypes, but to review them all would be a book in itself. It is still important to know and track all your numbers, though, and you can easily do this by signing up for a comprehensive testing service such as WellnessFX at their website, www.wellnessfx.com.

Saturated fats and trans fats, two unhealthy types of fats, typically lower your HDL cholesterol and increase your LDL cholesterol, therefore increasing plaque buildup. Unsaturated fats, such as monounsaturated omega-3 fatty acids, have been shown to have the opposite effect. In addition, while the bad fats and obesity have been shown to increase inflammation in the body—which is also associated with plaque buildup and other diseases such as cancer—these monounsaturated fatty acids have been shown to decrease inflammation. These unsaturated fats are most commonly found in fruits and vegetables in low concentrations, and fish in higher concentrations.

What You Should Eat

Understanding these basic concepts, you can now see why you would want to focus on eating lean protein, complex carbohydrates, and a limited amount of healthy fats—while trying to avoid unhealthy fats, sodium, and simple sugars. To do this, your diet should consist primarily of whole grains, fruits and vegetables, and lean protein and fish. In addition, you should try to avoid sweets, fried and fatty foods, and salty foods.

It is easy to think about all the foods that you should avoid, but that is not what will help you be successful in making the life change. Instead, think about all the delicious foods that can be prepared with the types of foods that are optimal for your health and energy. That is what this book will show you. Also think about the balanced weight, increased energy, and decreased risk of the effects and cost of disease on you and your family.

It's Not Just What, It's How Much

What distinguishes the DASH diet from just suggesting eating healthful foods is it offers an optimal amount of the types of foods to eat. Without knowing these amounts, it is easy to eat in excess. If you eat excessive amounts of any food, it will get stored as fat and contribute to obesity, which is unhealthy no matter which food contributed to it. The DASH diet suggests the following amounts:

- Whole Grains: 6–8 daily servings
- Lean Meats or Fish: 6 daily servings or less
- Vegetables: 4–5 daily servings
- Fruits: 4–5 daily servings
- Lean Dairy Products: 2–3 daily servings
- Fats and Oils: 2–3 daily servings or less
- Nuts, Seeds, or Legumes: 4–5 weekly servings
- Sweets and Added Sugars: 5 weekly servings or less

These servings vary based on your caloric needs, but the proportions should stay relatively the same. For example, if you are very active and burn about 3,000 calories per day, you may want to increase whole grains to 9–12 servings, fruits and vegetables to 6–8 servings each, and so on. Similarly, if you are highly inactive, you may want to reduce these amounts somewhat. However, in general, rather than reducing your intake you should—if possible—increase your activity and how many calories you use, as that has many other health benefits.

Putting It All Together

Whole grains, lean meats and fish, and fruits and vegetables are actively encouraged, while fats and sweets are limited. Throughout this book you will be given many examples of foods that fall into the categories of foods that are actively encouraged.

Lean dairy products are also encouraged. This is to ensure you receive an adequate amount of calcium. Of course, some people cannot consume dairy products for various reasons, such as lactose intolerance. In situations where you must avoid a certain food, you just need to understand which beneficial nutrients the food contains and how you can compensate for avoiding it. In the case of lean dairy products, because they supply protein and calcium, it is probably worth increasing lean meat intake slightly and taking a calcium supplement. To best understand what an individual food has that you may be lacking, you can start by reading the nutrition facts label. Here is an overall summary of the essential ingredients in the types of foods that are recommended:

- Whole Grains—Energy (carbohydrates) and fiber
- Fruits and Vegetables—Potassium, magnesium, and fiber
- Lean Dairy Products—Protein and calcium
- Lean Meats and Fish—Protein and essential fatty acids
- Nuts—Energy (carbohydrates and essential fatty acids), magnesium, potassium, and fiber

fact

The most important aspect of the DASH diet is eating more of certain types of foods and decreasing certain types of others. Following these basic principles will have a major impact on your health!

In addition to being a source of complex carbohydrates and a low amount of healthy fats, fruits and vegetables are also a rich source of vitamins and minerals. By eating more servings of fruits and vegetables, you ensure you get essential amounts of potassium and magnesium. Fruits and vegetables, such as whole grains and nuts, also give more fiber. Fiber is a type of carbohydrate that is linked in a way that cannot be absorbed into your bloodstream. Therefore, rather than causing a sugar spike, it attracts fluids into your gut through an osmosis-type effect that adds bulk to your stool and maintains colon health. As fiber is not absorbed, it can also reduce the absorption of cholesterol and improve your overall cholesterol profile.

What Not to Eat

Most of the foods that are recommended have a very limited amount of sodium, and so should decrease your salt intake. That decrease in salt is one of the biggest benefits of the DASH diet because as discussed, decreasing sodium can directly reduce blood pressure. To be sure that you are limiting your sodium intake, you can look at nutrition facts labels. In general, it is a good idea to start looking at nutrition facts labels more, as you will become better acquainted with the various ingredients in the food you eat, which is a huge step to informing and empowering yourself to take control of your health.

Salt

With sodium, the DASH diet actually has two different types of recommendations. The regular DASH diet suggests limiting sodium intake to 2,300 milligrams daily. If you eat the foods suggested in the DASH diet, you should be able to meet this goal without too much difficulty, but to be sure you can simply add up the sodium content of the various foods you eat to determine your daily total.

The alternative suggestion is for people at especially high risk, including middle-aged to elderly adults, African Americans, and those who already have high blood pressure. For these higher-risk groups, the recommended sodium intake is not to exceed 1,500 milligrams daily. This is a harder goal to meet without actively paying attention to sodium content, so if you do decide to follow this lower-sodium plan, it is especially important to pay attention to the total sodium on nutrition facts labels. In addition, if you fall into one of these categories and wish to try to follow the lower-sodium version of the plan, please make sure to talk to your doctor to ensure that such a plan is truly appropriate for you.

Alcohol

Another recommendation of the DASH diet is to limit alcohol intake. Alcohol is known to increase blood pressure and can worsen health. Some studies show a glass of wine daily can improve your cholesterol profile, but this limited benefit may be outweighed by the known harm. The official recommendation of the DASH diet is two or fewer drinks daily in men and one or fewer daily in women. Ultimately, though, as with sweets and fatty foods, the less alcohol you drink the healthier you will likely be.

Summary

Overall, the DASH diet is not intended to be a temporary change, but rather a sustainable lifestyle. Through the DASH diet, you can reduce your risk of many devastating diseases while achieving an ideal weight and giving yourself more energy. More benefits of the DASH diet are being discovered every day, and physicians and health institutes generally consider it the healthiest diet plan in existence. You have completed the vital task of learning about the DASH diet, and the rest of this book will guide you with delicious recipes to help implement it. You do not need to strictly follow the DASH diet from the first day, as the DASH diet allows gradual change, and forgiveness of imperfection. The DASH diet is a journey, so congratulations on completing the first step.

Breakfast

Swiss Cheese and Chive Mini Quiches

MAKES 12

Per Serving (2 mini quiches):

Calories	170
Fat	7g
Sodium	93mg
Carbohydrates	18g
Fiber	1g
Sugar	2g
Protein	7g

These tasty treats look impressive, but require very little preparation and equipment—all you need is a rolling pin and muffin tin. Feel free to vary the ingredients according to mood and season.

¾ cup plus 2 tablespoons unbleached all-purpose flour, divided

½ teaspoon salt-free all-purpose seasoning

¼ teaspoon dried dill

2 tablespoons unsalted butter

2 large eggs

⅔ cup low-fat milk

⅓ cup nonfat or low-fat sour cream

6 tablespoons shredded Swiss cheese

¼ cup chopped fresh chives

¼ teaspoon ground black pepper

1 Preheat oven to 350°F. Spray a muffin tin with nonstick cooking spray.

2 Place ¾ cup flour, all-purpose seasoning, and dill in a large bowl and whisk to combine. Add butter and use a pastry cutter, two knives, or your fingers to cut it into the flour mixture until the mixture resembles fine crumbs.

3 Add cold water, ½ tablespoon at a time, until the dough just comes together. Roll the dough out thinly and cut into 12 (2") circles using a biscuit cutter or a drinking glass.

4 Line each cup of the prepared muffin tin with a round of dough and set aside.

5 Beat eggs, milk, sour cream, and the remaining 2 tablespoons flour in a medium bowl until combined.

6 Divide mixture evenly among the muffin tin cups. Top each quiche with ½ tablespoon shredded Swiss cheese and 1 teaspoon chives. Sprinkle with pepper.

7 Place pan on middle rack in oven and bake for 25 minutes. Remove from oven and let it rest for a few minutes. Remove mini quiches by sliding a knife around edges and gently lifting up. Serve warm or at room temperature.

Maple Turkey Sausage

Perfect for those avoiding pork or simply looking for another lean breakfast meat, these homemade patties are subtly sweet and absolutely delicious.

2 pounds lean ground turkey

1 large egg white

1 tablespoon maple syrup

1 tablespoon ground sage

½ teaspoon dried red pepper flakes

½ teaspoon fennel seed

½ teaspoon ground black pepper

½ teaspoon ground rosemary

¼ teaspoon garlic powder

1 Combine all ingredients in a large bowl and mix using a fork or your hands. The mixture will be sticky. Form into 16 (2") patties.

2 Heat a griddle or skillet over medium heat and brown patties on both sides, about 4 minutes per side. Reduce heat to medium-low or low if the patties seem to be burning. Drain on paper towels before serving.

Scrambled Tofu with Mushrooms, Peppers, and Tomatoes

This is a great salt-free dish, especially good for vegans or those watching their cholesterol, and the taste is surprisingly authentic. Adapted from a recipe by Christina Pirello. Many thanks to Christina for passing it along!

1 small onion, peeled and diced

1 clove garlic, peeled and minced

1 cup sliced mushrooms

1 small tomato, diced

1 small bell pepper, seeded and diced

1 pound firm or extra-firm tofu, drained

½ teaspoon salt-free all-purpose seasoning

½ teaspoon ground black pepper

½ teaspoon ground turmeric

1 Place a large nonstick skillet over medium heat. Add onion, garlic, mushrooms, tomato, and bell pepper and cook, stirring, for 5 minutes.

2 Crumble tofu over the vegetable mixture, keeping it in rather large chunks. Add salt-free seasoning, black pepper, and turmeric and stir gently to combine. Cook another 5 minutes, stirring gently.

3 Remove from heat and serve immediately.

SERVES 4	
Per Serving:	
Calories	124
Fat	6g
Sodium	7mg
Carbohydrates	6g
Fiber	2g
Sugar	1g
Protein	12g

WHAT IS TURMERIC?

Turmeric is a spice made from the ground root of the turmeric plant. Its bright yellow color and distinct flavor are used in many types of food, from Indian cuisine to prepared mustard. Turmeric has a slightly bitter taste that works well in combination with other seasonings. It's high in manganese and iron, and may help reduce the risk of some cancers.

Scrambled Eggs with Apples, Sage, and Swiss

SERVES 2

Per Serving:

Calories	165
Fat	8g
Sodium	97mg
Carbohydrates	12g
Fiber	2g
Sugar	8g
Protein	10g

This combination of tastes and textures seems tailor-made for fall: the warmth and softness of the eggs, the tang of the Swiss, the play of apple against shallot, and the sage—don't forget the sage! That woodsy scent draws everything together.

2 large eggs

1 medium apple, cored and chopped

1 small shallot, peeled and chopped

¼ cup shredded Swiss cheese

1 teaspoon chopped fresh sage or ½ teaspoon dried sage

¼ teaspoon ground black pepper

1 Beat eggs in a small bowl; set aside.

2 Place a medium nonstick skillet over medium-low heat. Add apple and shallot and cook, stirring, until soft but not brown, 3–5 minutes.

3 Add egg. Let set for 30 seconds, then cook, stirring, 30 seconds to 1 minute more, until egg is almost cooked. Add cheese and stir.

4 Remove from heat and serve immediately, sprinkled with sage and pepper.

Diner-Style Home Fries

Tender, seasoned potatoes sautéed with onion and bell pepper make the most delicious side dish at breakfast.

4 medium potatoes, peeled and cut into ½" cubes

1 teaspoon olive oil

1 medium onion, peeled and diced

1 medium sweet bell pepper, seeded and diced

1 tablespoon no-salt-added tomato paste

2 teaspoons ground paprika

½ teaspoon dried thyme

½ teaspoon garlic powder

½ teaspoon dried rosemary

¼ teaspoon ground black pepper

1 Place potatoes in a medium microwave-safe bowl and cover with microwave-safe plastic wrap. Microwave for 7 minutes.

2 While potatoes are cooking, heat oil in a large nonstick skillet over medium heat. Add onion and bell pepper and cook, stirring, for 7 minutes.

3 Add cooked potatoes, tomato paste, paprika, thyme, garlic powder, rosemary, and black pepper. Stir to combine, then cook, stirring, another 2–3 minutes. Remove from heat and serve.

SERVES 6

Per Serving:	
Calories	101
Fat	1g
Sodium	10mg
Carbohydrates	21g
Fiber	2g
Sugar	2g
Protein	2g

VARIATIONS ON A THEME

Home fries and hashes make an easy and inexpensive breakfast and can be crafted using almost anything. Instead of standard potatoes, try making home fries with sweet potatoes, crumbled low-sodium bacon, and leeks. Dice leftover meat, hard-boiled eggs, and/or low-sodium cheese and add to the mix. Or shred a big variety of vegetables and make yourself a super vegan hash.

Homemade Granola

Subtly sweet and super crunchy, this cereal keeps well for weeks when stored in an airtight container. The dried fruit is stirred in after the cereal has fully cooled, so it stays soft. Unsweetened shredded coconut lends a lot of flavor without much sodium; eliminate if you're watching your fat.

MAKES 10 CUPS

Per Serving (½ cup):

Calories	266
Fat	10g
Sodium	7mg
Carbohydrates	42g
Fiber	4g
Sugar	19g
Protein	5g

6 cups quick or old-fashioned oats

1¼ cups unsalted chopped walnuts or almonds

½ cup dried unsweetened shredded coconut

1 teaspoon ground cinnamon

½ teaspoon ground ginger

¼ teaspoon ground cloves

¼ teaspoon ground nutmeg

1 cup maple syrup

1½ tablespoons vanilla extract

2 cups chopped mixed dried fruit

1 Preheat oven to 350°F. Spray two large rimmed baking sheets with nonstick cooking spray and set aside.

2 In a large bowl, combine oats, nuts, coconut, cinnamon, ginger, cloves, and nutmeg.

3 Add maple syrup and vanilla and stir until everything is thoroughly coated.

4 Divide the mixture between the prepared baking sheets. Place the sheets on the middle rack in the oven and bake until golden brown, 25–30 minutes. Two or three times during baking, remove baking sheets and carefully stir contents. This will ensure even baking so granola does not burn.

5 Remove baking sheets from the oven and set aside to cool fully. Stir dried fruit into the mixture. Store in an airtight container.

5-Spice Quinoa with Apples and Raisins

This simple, hot, and filling breakfast is especially great in fall and winter. Keep the peel on the apple for added nutrients and fiber. If you prefer softer fruit, add it during the cooking time rather than after.

1 cup quinoa

1 cup water

1 cup unsweetened apple juice

½ teaspoon ground 5-spice powder

1 medium apple, peeled, cored, and chopped

¼ cup raisins

SERVES 4	
Per Serving:	
Calories	207
Fat	2g
Sodium	11mg
Carbohydrates	43g
Fiber	4g
Sugar	16g
Protein	5g

1 Measure quinoa, water, apple juice, and 5-spice powder into a medium saucepan. Bring to a boil over high heat.

2 Reduce heat to medium-low, cover pan, and simmer for 15 minutes.

3 Remove from heat, stir in apple and raisins, and serve immediately.

Coconut Rice with Dried Apricots and Mint

This sweet rice makes a scrumptious alternative to oatmeal at breakfast. Omit the agave nectar if you prefer it less sweet. Try adding chopped nuts and serving it as a side dish at dinner as well.

¾ cup light coconut milk

¼ cup water

½ cup basmati rice, rinsed

1 tablespoon agave nectar

⅓ cup diced dried apricots

⅛ teaspoon ground cardamom

1 tablespoon chopped fresh mint

1 Combine coconut milk and water in a 3-quart saucepan. Bring to a boil over high heat.

2 Add rice, reduce heat to low, cover, and simmer for 15 minutes.

3 Remove pan from heat. Stir in agave nectar, dried apricots, cardamom, and mint. Serve immediately.

SERVES 4

Per Serving:

Calories	118
Fat	3g
Sodium	10mg
Carbohydrates	20g
Fiber	1g
Sugar	8g
Protein	1g

WHAT IS AGAVE NECTAR?

Agave nectar is a liquid sweetener derived from the agave cactus. It's a clear, light brown liquid, similar in look to maple syrup, although slightly thicker. It has a subtle, pleasant flavor and is very sweet, about twice as sweet as cane sugar. Because of its liquid form, it dissolves instantly, making it a great choice for sweetening beverages and dressings. Unlike honey, agave nectar is a strictly vegan food.

Hot Honey Porridge

Warm and filling, this healthy multigrain cereal has a soft honey taste and a creamy, slightly chewy texture. Add dried fruit or chopped nuts if you like.

¾ cup bulgur wheat

½ cup rolled oats

3 cups boiling water

¼ cup honey

1 Place bulgur and oats in a medium saucepan. Add boiling water and stir to combine.

2 Place pan over high heat and bring to a boil. Reduce heat to low, cover, and simmer for 10 minutes, stirring occasionally.

3 Remove from heat, stir in honey, and serve immediately.

Whole-Wheat Cinnamon Pancakes with Banana

These delicious pancakes—flavored with ripe banana, cinnamon, and vanilla—make a fabulous low-fat breakfast.

1⅓ cups white whole-wheat flour

¼ cup sugar

1 tablespoon sodium-free baking powder

1⅓ cups low-fat milk

1 large egg white

1 teaspoon ground cinnamon

1 tablespoon vanilla extract

1 medium banana, peeled and sliced

SERVES 4	
Per Serving:	
Calories	274
Fat	1g
Sodium	53mg
Carbohydrates	54g
Fiber	6g
Sugar	21g
Protein	9g

1 Measure flour, sugar, and baking powder into a large bowl and whisk to combine.

2 Add milk, egg white, cinnamon, and vanilla. Mix and let sit for 1–2 minutes to thicken.

3 Heat a nonstick griddle or medium skillet over medium heat. Pour ¼ of the batter onto the heated griddle. Arrange ¼ of the banana slices over top. When pancake has bubbled on top and is nicely browned on bottom (2–4 minutes), flip over.

4 Brown on the second side for another 2–3 minutes. Transfer cooked pancake to a plate.

5 Repeat the process with the remaining batter. Serve warm.

Oven-Baked Apple Pancake

Moist, airy, and delicious, this cholesterol-free pancake will impress with its taste and simplicity. Just whisk together the ingredients, pour, and bake. The oven does all of the work.

SERVES 8

Per Serving:

Calories	126
Fat	1g
Sodium	10mg
Carbohydrates	27g
Fiber	1g
Sugar	13g
Protein	2g

CHOICES, CHOICES

There's a nondairy milk for every taste, from soy and rice milks to almond, coconut, hemp, oat, and more. Plain, sweetened, and even flavored varieties exist. Don't know which to try? Sample different brands, varieties, and flavors until you find one or more you enjoy. You can even make your own nondairy milk at home. It's not hard, but is best made using a super-strong blender, such as Vitamix.

2 cups diced apple

1 tablespoon vanilla extract

1 tablespoon sodium-free baking powder

1 cup unbleached all-purpose flour

⅓ cup unsweetened applesauce

⅓ cup maple syrup

¾ cup nondairy milk

1 tablespoon sugar

½ teaspoon ground cinnamon

1. Preheat oven to 400°F. Lightly spray a large ovenproof skillet with nonstick cooking spray.
2. Place apple, vanilla, baking powder, flour, applesauce, maple syrup, and nondairy milk in a large bowl and stir to combine. Pour batter into the prepared skillet and smooth the top.
3. Combine sugar and cinnamon in a small bowl and sprinkle evenly over the batter.
4. Place skillet on middle rack in oven and bake for 25 minutes. Remove from oven. Carefully loosen pancake from skillet using a spatula. Slice into 8 wedges and serve immediately.

Orange Cornmeal Pancakes

These light, fluffy pancakes are so good, you may even pass on the syrup.

2/3 cup white whole-wheat flour

2/3 cup cornmeal

1 tablespoon sodium-free baking powder

1/4 cup sugar

3 tablespoons orange juice

1½ teaspoons grated orange zest

1 cup low-fat milk

1 large egg white

SERVES 4	
Per Serving:	
Calories	223
Fat	2g
Sodium	48mg
Carbohydrates	46g
Fiber	4g
Sugar	16g
Protein	7g

1 Stir together all ingredients in a medium bowl.

2 Heat a nonstick griddle or medium skillet over medium-low heat. Pour spoonfuls of batter onto the heated griddle. When pancakes have bubbled on top and are nicely browned on bottom, about 2 minutes, flip over and cook 2 minutes more. Transfer cooked pancakes to a plate.

3 Repeat with remaining batter. Serve immediately.

Sweet Potato Breakfast Pie

A cross between hash browns and a pancake, this super-healthy, oven-baked breakfast will garner rave reviews. Serve plain or drizzled lightly with maple syrup.

2 cups shredded sweet potato

1 cup shredded carrot

¼ cup white whole-wheat flour

2 large egg whites

1 tablespoon maple syrup

1 tablespoon orange juice

½ teaspoon grated orange zest

¼ teaspoon ground cinnamon

1 Preheat oven to 425°F. Spray a pie pan lightly with nonstick cooking spray and set aside.

2 Place all ingredients in a large bowl and stir to combine. Spread mixture in the prepared pan and smooth the top.

3 Place pan on the middle rack in oven and bake for 20 minutes. Remove from oven and cut into wedges. Serve warm.

Sunday Morning Waffles

Homemade waffles make a simple but impressive breakfast. As a bonus, they freeze beautifully, so you can make them in bulk, store them in the freezer, and then toast them for quick weekday breakfasts.

1⅔ cups unbleached all-purpose flour

¼ cup sugar

1 tablespoon sodium-free baking powder

2 large egg whites

1½ cups low-fat milk

2 teaspoons vanilla extract

2 tablespoons canola oil

1 Place flour, sugar, and baking powder in a large bowl and whisk to combine.
2 Place egg whites in a medium bowl and beat until they form stiff peaks.
3 Stir in milk, vanilla, and oil to the flour mixture. Set aside for 1–2 minutes to thicken, then gently fold beaten egg whites into the batter.
4 Heat a waffle iron. Spray lightly with nonstick cooking spray, then ladle batter onto the hot surface, being careful to avoid the edges. Close waffle iron and bake until golden brown, 4–5 minutes.
5 Remove baked waffle from the iron and repeat the process with remaining batter. Serve immediately.

SERVES 6

Per Serving:

Calories	220
Fat	6g
Sodium	46mg
Carbohydrates	35g
Fiber	4g
Sugar	11g
Protein	7g

WAFFLE TIP

After removing waffles from the waffle iron, place them directly on the middle rack of a preheated 200°F oven until all the waffles are done. When serving, do not stack the waffles. The moisture from the waffles will condense and cause waffles to become limp. Always serve waffles in a single layer to keep them fresh and crisp.

Whole-Grain Spiced Pear Waffles

SERVES 8

Per Serving:

Calories	297
Fat	14g
Sodium	34mg
Carbohydrates	38g
Fiber	5g
Sugar	16g
Protein	9g

Crisp and hearty, these healthy waffles are also great with chopped apple and pecans.

2 medium pears, peeled, cored, and diced, divided

1⅔ cups white whole-wheat flour

⅓ cup sugar

1½ tablespoons sodium-free baking powder

2 cups low-fat milk

1 large egg white

2 tablespoons canola oil

2 teaspoons vanilla extract

1 teaspoon ground cinnamon

½ teaspoon ground ginger

¼ teaspoon ground nutmeg

1 cup chopped walnuts, divided

1 Measure ½ cup diced pears and set aside. Place remaining pears in a large bowl.

2 Add flour, sugar, baking powder, milk, egg white, oil, vanilla, cinnamon, ginger, nutmeg, and ½ cup walnuts to the bowl and beat until smooth.

3 Heat a waffle iron. Spray lightly with nonstick cooking spray, then ladle batter onto the hot surface, being careful to avoid the edges. Close waffle iron and bake until golden brown, 4–5 minutes.

4 Remove baked waffle from the iron and repeat process with remaining batter. Top waffles with reserved ½ cup pears and remaining ½ cup walnuts. Serve immediately.

ABC Muffins

MAKES 12

Per Serving (1 muffin):

Calories	128
Fat	4g
Sodium	11mg
Carbohydrates	22g
Fiber	2g
Sugar	9g
Protein	2g

SODIUM-FREE BAKING POWDER

Standard baking powder, the kind typically sold in supermarkets, contains hundreds of milligrams of sodium per serving and is not recommended on the DASH diet. Two brands of sodium-free baking powder are available and provide the same great rise in baked goods. Ener-G sodium-free baking powder can be purchased online. Featherweight sodium-free baking powder is sold online, at Whole Foods Market shops, and other select stores.

Apple, banana, and carrot give these muffins superb moistness and flavor. Packed with vitamins and nutrients, they make a great cholesterol-free breakfast or quick snack.

2 medium apples, cored and chopped

2 medium carrots, peeled and shredded

1 medium banana, peeled and mashed

3 tablespoons canola oil

¼ cup almond or soy milk

¼ cup light brown sugar

1 tablespoon vanilla extract

1 cup unbleached all-purpose flour

¼ cup white whole-wheat flour

1½ teaspoons sodium-free baking powder

1 Preheat oven to 350°F. Spray a twelve-cup muffin tin lightly with nonstick cooking spray or line with paper liners. Set aside.

2 Place all ingredients in a large bowl and mix.

3 Divide batter evenly among the muffin cups. Place tin on middle rack in oven and bake for 20–25 minutes.

4 Remove from oven and place tin on a wire rack to cool. Cool fully before removing muffins from tin and eating.

Whole-Wheat Strawberry Corn Muffins

The combination of plump, moist berries and the subtle crunch of cornmeal is irresistible in these fabulous vegan muffins.

1 cup white whole-wheat flour

½ cup cornmeal

½ cup sugar

1 tablespoon sodium-free baking powder

1 cup chopped strawberries

1 cup nondairy milk

3 tablespoons canola oil

2 teaspoons vanilla extract

MAKES 12

Per Serving (1 muffin):

Calories	128
Fat	4g
Sodium	10mg
Carbohydrates	21g
Fiber	2g
Sugar	9g
Protein	2g

1 Preheat oven to 375°F. Line a twelve-cup muffin tin with paper liners and set aside.

2 Place flour, cornmeal, sugar, and baking powder in a large bowl and whisk to combine.

3 Add strawberries, milk, oil, and vanilla and stir until incorporated.

4 Fill each muffin cup ⅔ full. Place muffin tin on middle rack in oven and bake for 20 minutes.

5 Remove from oven and place on a wire rack to cool. Let muffins cool at least 10 minutes before serving to ensure paper wrappers come off with ease.

Maple, Oatmeal, and Applesauce Muffins

MAKES 12

Per Serving (1 muffin):

Calories	164
Fat	5g
Sodium	16mg
Carbohydrates	26g
Fiber	1g
Sugar	11g
Protein	3g

LOW-SODIUM AND SODIUM-FREE PRODUCTS

The DASH diet requires you to purchase some specialty items, such as low-sodium baking powder and baking soda, that may not be available in local stores. Two online sources of these and many other low-sodium products are www .healthyheartmarket .com.

With all the comforting flavor of a bowl of oatmeal in a convenient package, these yummy muffins make any busy morning better. Bake a batch ahead of time, freeze, and then pop one out the night before to thaw.

1 cup low-fat milk

1 tablespoon distilled white vinegar

1 cup old-fashioned rolled oats

1 large egg white

¼ cup canola oil

¼ cup unsweetened applesauce

⅓ cup light brown sugar

¼ cup maple syrup

1 teaspoon ground cinnamon

2 teaspoons sodium-free baking powder

1 teaspoon sodium-free baking soda

1 cup unbleached all-purpose flour

¼ cup whole-wheat flour

1. Preheat oven to 425°F. Grease a twelve-cup muffin tin or line with paper liners. Set aside.
2. Pour milk into a measuring cup and add vinegar. Set aside for 5 minutes. Pour mixture into a large bowl and stir in oats. Set aside for 10 minutes.
3. Add egg white, oil, and applesauce to the oat mixture and stir. Stir in brown sugar, maple syrup, cinnamon, baking powder, and baking soda.
4. Gradually add all-purpose and whole-wheat flours and stir to combine.
5. Pour the batter into the muffin cups, dividing evenly. Place pan on the middle rack in the preheated oven and bake for 20–25 minutes.
6. Remove pan from oven, then carefully remove muffins from cups and place on a wire rack to cool.

CHAPTER 3

Appetizers and Snacks

Coconut-Crusted Chicken with Spicy-Sweet Dipping Sauce

SERVES 6

Per Serving:

Calories	105
Fat	4g
Sodium	39mg
Carbohydrates	10g
Fiber	1g
Sugar	5g
Protein	7g

Deliciously crisp breading gives way to moist and tender chicken in this healthier alternative to coconut shrimp. A tasty vegan version can be made using 8 ounces of tempeh instead of chicken and egg replacement powder. Tempeh cooks quicker than chicken; it will only need about 15 minutes total in the oven.

¼ cup unsweetened coconut

¼ cup salt-free bread crumbs

1 teaspoon garlic powder

¼ teaspoon ground black pepper

1 large egg white

4 boneless, skinless chicken thighs, cut into bite-sized pieces

2 tablespoons orange marmalade

1½ teaspoons unflavored rice vinegar

¼ teaspoon dried red pepper flakes

1 Preheat oven to 425°F. Spray a baking sheet lightly with nonstick cooking spray and set aside.

2 Measure coconut, bread crumbs, garlic powder, and black pepper into a small bowl and whisk to combine.

3 Beat egg white in a shallow bowl.

4 Dip each piece of chicken into the egg, then coat with bread crumbs. Place on prepared baking sheet. Place baking sheet on middle rack in oven and bake 10 minutes.

5 Flip chicken and return to oven for another 10 minutes.

6 While chicken is baking, combine marmalade, vinegar, and red pepper flakes in a small bowl and stir to combine.

7 Remove baking sheet from oven and transfer chicken to a platter, along with the dipping sauce. Serve immediately.

Vegetable Sushi

Although it looks complicated, sushi is simple and inexpensive to make, requiring nothing more than the ingredients, a flexible bamboo sushi mat, and a sharp knife. Dry sheets of nori seaweed are sold in the Asian aisle of most supermarkets. Sushi rice, sometimes called sticky rice, should also be there.

2 cups sushi rice

3 cups water

1 medium carrot

1 medium cucumber

2 tablespoons unflavored rice vinegar

5 sheets unflavored nori

1 Place rice and water in a medium saucepan and bring to a boil over high heat. Reduce heat to low, cover, and simmer for 20 minutes.

2 While rice is cooking, peel carrot and cucumber. Remove cucumber seeds by halving lengthwise, then gently scraping out seeds with a spoon. Slice carrot and cucumber into thin matchsticks or strips and set aside.

3 When rice is done, remove from heat. Stir in vinegar.

4 Take out a sheet of nori. One side should be shinier than the other; place the shiny side down on the bamboo mat. Spread a thin layer of rice (about ¼" thick) over the top, leaving a 1" bare lip near you and about 2" bare on the far edge.

5 Place a few strips of carrot and cucumber on top of the rice, 2"–3" from the bare edge closest to you. Lightly wet the bare edges, then carefully roll the nori away from you, pressing firmly to seal. Continue rolling to the far edge, then roll back and forth to seal completely.

6 Using a very sharp knife, slice the roll into 6 equal segments, dipping the knife into the water and cleaning off the blade between cuts to prevent sticking. Repeat with remaining ingredients.

7 Serve sushi immediately or cover and refrigerate until serving.

SERVES 6

Per Serving:

Calories	73
Fat	0g
Sodium	15mg
Carbohydrates	15g
Fiber	1g
Sugar	2g
Protein	2g

SUSHI TIP

When making sushi, position a bowl of water nearby on the counter. Dip your sticky fingers into the water to make rice arrangement easier, and use it to rinse your knife for clean and pressure-free slicing.

Zucchini Sticks

Modeled after fried mozzarella, these yummy zucchini sticks are crisp and golden on the outside and tender inside.

1 large egg white

1 tablespoon water

3 tablespoons salt-free bread crumbs

1 tablespoon grated Parmesan cheese

1 teaspoon salt-free Italian seasoning

½ teaspoon garlic powder

½ teaspoon onion powder

¼ teaspoon ground black pepper

⅛ teaspoon ground paprika

2 medium zucchini, trimmed and cut into long wedges

½ cup no-salt-added pasta sauce

1 Preheat oven to 450°F. Spray a baking sheet lightly with nonstick cooking spray and set aside.

2 Beat egg white and water in a small shallow bowl. Set aside.

3 Place bread crumbs, cheese, Italian seasoning, garlic powder, onion powder, pepper, and paprika in a small bowl and whisk to combine.

4 Dip each piece of zucchini in egg white mixture, then roll in bread crumbs. Place on the prepared baking sheet. Place baking sheet on middle rack in oven and bake for 15 minutes.

5 While zucchini is baking, gently warm pasta sauce in a small saucepan over medium-low heat for 5 minutes. Pour into a small bowl and set aside.

6 Remove zucchini from oven and serve immediately with warm sauce.

SERVES 6

Per Serving:

Calories	39
Fat	1g
Sodium	28mg
Carbohydrates	6g
Fiber	1g
Sugar	2g
Protein	2g

FOR THE LOVE OF ZUCCHINI

Easy to grow and notoriously prodigious, zucchini is a garden favorite. When planting, leave plenty of space for the specimens to spread. The leaves of zucchini plants and the vegetables themselves can grow to massive proportions. Zucchini are best harvested when young and tender; older specimens can become tough and unappealing. The flowers of the plant are also edible. Many farmers' markets now offer zucchini blossoms for sale; keep an eye out when shopping.

Spice-Rubbed Chicken Wings

SERVES 6

Per Serving:

Calories	464
Fat	18g
Sodium	185mg
Carbohydrates	1g
Fiber	0g
Sugar	0g
Protein	64g

WASTE NOT, WANT NOT

Animal bones can't be composted, but they can be used to flavor recipes, especially homemade broth. Place bones and other scraps in a stockpot, add water, and bring to a boil over high heat. Reduce heat to low, cover, and simmer an hour or more. When it comes to vegetable trimmings, do the same. Peels, leaves, and stems may be unappealing to eat, but add a lot of flavor to stock. Save discarded scraps in plastic bags, seal, and freeze for later use.

These flavorful wings are great for casual parties or game-day get-togethers. The spice rub works well on other cuts of chicken, from thighs to drumsticks, and even whole birds. For more heat, add a pinch of ground cayenne pepper to the blend.

2 teaspoons ground cumin

1 teaspoon ground coriander

1 teaspoon ground mustard

1 teaspoon garlic powder

1 teaspoon onion powder

½ teaspoon ground black pepper

¼ teaspoon dried red pepper flakes

¼ teaspoon ground paprika

3 pounds chicken wings

1 Place cumin, coriander, mustard, garlic powder, onion powder, black pepper, red pepper flakes, and paprika in a small bowl and whisk to combine.
2 Rub wings all over with spice mixture. Place wings in a large bowl, cover, and refrigerate several hours or overnight.
3 When ready to cook, heat grill to medium heat or preheat oven to 450°F.
4 If grilling, place wings on grates and grill 20 minutes, flipping frequently to prevent burning. Keep wings away from direct flame. The wings are done when an internal temperature of 180°F is reached.
5 If roasting in oven, place wings on a lightly oiled baking sheet. Place sheet on middle rack in oven and bake 15 minutes. Flip the wings, return to oven, and bake another 15 minutes.
6 Serve immediately.

Savory Stuffed Mushrooms

A lovely appetizer or light nosh, these stuffed mushrooms have a crisp and tasty breading that's so good, they'll be gone before you know it.

16 ounces button or baby bella mushrooms

2 tablespoons olive oil

½ cup salt-free bread crumbs

1 large egg white

½ cup shredded Swiss cheese

4 cloves garlic, peeled

1 teaspoon salt-free Italian seasoning

½ teaspoon ground black pepper

SERVES 6	
Per Serving:	
Calories	124
Fat	7g
Sodium	30mg
Carbohydrates	10g
Fiber	1g
Sugar	1g
Protein	5g

1 Preheat oven to 400°F. Spray a baking sheet lightly with nonstick cooking spray and set aside.

2 Clean mushrooms and gently remove stems, taking care to leave caps intact. Set caps aside.

3 Place mushroom stems in a food processor and add the remaining ingredients. Pulse several times to finely chop and combine the mixture.

4 Stuff mushroom caps with the mixture, then place on the prepared baking sheet. Place baking sheet on middle rack in oven and bake 15 minutes. Remove from oven.

5 Mushrooms can be served warm or at room temperature.

Baked Tofu with Tangy Dipping Sauce

Per Serving:

Calories	121
Fat	3g
Sodium	15mg
Carbohydrates	15g
Fiber	2g
Sugar	6g
Protein	8g

WHAT IS TOFU?

Tofu is made from soybeans in a process not unlike the making of cheese. Bean curds are separated from liquid and pressed into blocks. Tofu is sold in two main types. The first type, what many consider "regular" tofu, is sold in blocks submerged in liquid. It comes in silken, firm, and extra-firm varieties and must be kept refrigerated. The second type of tofu, which comes in shelf-stable packaging and does not need to be refrigerated, is silken style. It comes in varying levels of firmness, from silken to extra firm; all have a soft, smooth feel.

Anything but bland, these breaded, oven-fried cutlets will make a tofu lover out of you! Paired with a sweet, slightly spicy sauce, they're absolutely delicious. Double the recipe for larger parties.

1 pound extra-firm tofu, drained

1 large egg white

1 tablespoon water

½ cup salt-free bread crumbs

1 tablespoon dried parsley

1 teaspoon salt-free Italian seasoning

1 teaspoon ground paprika

1 teaspoon onion powder

½ teaspoon garlic powder

½ teaspoon ground black pepper

1 (8-ounce) can no-salt-added tomato sauce

1 tablespoon apple cider vinegar

1 tablespoon molasses

1 tablespoon honey

1 tablespoon ground mustard

½ teaspoon ground cumin

⅛ teaspoon ground cayenne pepper

1 Preheat oven to 425°F. Spray a baking sheet lightly with nonstick cooking spray and set aside.

2 Gently press tofu between paper towels to release excess liquid. Slice tofu in half lengthwise, then slice each half into 8 equal pieces.

3 Beat egg white and water in a shallow bowl until slightly foamy.

4 Place bread crumbs, parsley, Italian seasoning, paprika, onion powder, garlic powder, and black pepper in a shallow bowl and whisk to combine.

5 Dip each piece of tofu in egg white, then gently press in bread crumb mixture to coat. Place coated tofu cutlets on prepared baking sheet.

6 Place baking sheet on middle rack in oven and bake 10 minutes. Remove from oven, gently flip cutlets, and return to oven to bake another 10 minutes.

7 While tofu is baking, combine tomato sauce, vinegar, molasses, honey, mustard, cumin, and cayenne in a small saucepan. Heat over medium-low heat, stirring frequently. Once mixture begins to bubble, remove from heat and pour into a small serving bowl.

8 Remove tofu from oven and serve immediately with dipping sauce.

Sweet and Spicy Salt-Free Pickles

With a brine this sassy, you won't notice the lack of salt, and it's great for pickling other vegetables too. The flavor increases the longer the cucumbers marinate, so these are best made at least a day before serving.

3 large cucumbers, sliced into thin rounds

1 medium onion, peeled and thinly sliced

6 cloves garlic, peeled and minced

4 cups white vinegar

2 cups sugar

1 tablespoon mustard seed

3 bay leaves

1 teaspoon dried red pepper flakes

½ teaspoon whole peppercorns

1 Place cucumbers, onion, and garlic in a large lidded jar or other airtight container.

2 Combine vinegar, sugar, mustard seed, bay leaves, red pepper flakes, and peppercorns in a medium saucepan and stir to combine. Bring to a boil over medium heat, stirring occasionally. Remove from heat and pour over mixture in jar.

3 Screw on lid and set aside until cool.

4 Store in refrigerator. Pickles will keep for several weeks in refrigerator.

MAKES 10 CUPS

Per Serving (¼ cup):

Calories	23
Fat	0g
Sodium	2mg
Carbohydrates	4g
Fiber	0g
Sugar	3g
Protein	0g

Crunchy Coated Nuts

SERVES 8

Per Serving:

Calories	226
Fat	17g
Sodium	13mg
Carbohydrates	14g
Fiber	3g
Sugar	5g
Protein	6g

HEALTHY HOMEMADE GIFTS

The most thoughtful gifts are often those you make yourself. Packaging unsalted nuts and other salt-free snacks in tins or glass containers is a tasty way of showing you care. At holiday time, there's nothing sweeter than sharing a tray of healthy, home-baked sweets. And remember, salt-free seasonings and condiments are practical as well as delicious. Placed in a pretty jar or squeeze bottle, they're a gift that keeps on giving.

Slightly sweet, with a spicy kick from the cayenne, these crunchy nuts are the life of any party. If you prefer less heat, reduce the amount of cayenne pepper. Recipe adapted from Food Network Kitchens Favorite Recipes.

1 large egg white

3 tablespoons light brown sugar

2 teaspoons dried oregano

¾ teaspoon ground coriander

½ teaspoon ground cumin

¼ teaspoon ground cayenne pepper

⅛ teaspoon ground cloves

2 cups unsalted mixed nuts

1 Preheat oven to 300°F. Line a rimmed baking sheet with parchment paper or foil.
2 Place egg white, brown sugar, oregano, coriander, cumin, cayenne, and cloves in a medium bowl and whisk until combined.
3 Add nuts and toss until evenly coated.
4 Arrange nuts in a single layer on the prepared baking sheet.
5 Place baking sheet on the middle rack in oven and bake 30 minutes, removing the baking sheet halfway through baking time, stirring, and returning to oven.
6 Remove baking sheet from oven and set on a wire rack to cool. Nuts will crisp as they dry and cool, so let them cool fully before removing from the sheet. Store in an airtight container for up to 5 days.

Cheesy Seasoned Popcorn

This seasoned popcorn will satisfy salty snack cravings anytime. Experiment with different herbs or try a sugar and spice blend.

2 tablespoons nutritional yeast flakes

1½ teaspoons dried dill

1 teaspoon dried parsley

¾ teaspoon garlic powder

¾ teaspoon onion powder

½ teaspoon ground paprika

¼ teaspoon dried thyme

¼ teaspoon ground black pepper

½ cup popcorn kernels

2 teaspoons olive oil

MAKES 10 CUPS	
Per Serving (1 cup):	
Calories	55
Fat	1g
Sodium	2mg
Carbohydrates	8g
Fiber	2g
Sugar	<1g
Protein	2g

1 Combine nutritional yeast, dill, parsley, garlic powder, onion powder, paprika, thyme, and black pepper in a small bowl and stir. Set aside.

2 Place popcorn kernels in an air popper. Place a large stockpot beneath the popcorn dispenser, turn on appliance, and wait until all kernels have popped. Turn off popper and set aside.

3 Drizzle oil over popcorn and toss to coat. Sprinkle with the nutritional yeast mixture and stir vigorously for several minutes until completely coated.

4 Serve immediately or store in an airtight container until serving.

Mushroom, Swiss, and Jalapeño Quesadillas

Per Serving:

Calories	192
Fat	6g
Sodium	103mg
Carbohydrates	28g
Fiber	2g
Sugar	2g
Protein	10g

GARDEN CITY ALL NATURAL LAVASH ROLL-UPS

Sold at Whole Foods Market, these round tortilla-like wraps are a perfect choice for low-sodium dieters. They're sold in white or whole-wheat versions, and contain a mere 20 milligrams of sodium per serving. Garden City lavash are usually stocked in the bakery department near the bread.

What could be better than lightly grilled tortillas with a spicy, cheesy, savory filling? Perfect as appetizers or a light meal, these quesadillas leave processed fast food in the dust, where it should be. If spicy food is not your thing, simply omit the jalapeño.

1 teaspoon olive oil

1 pound white mushrooms, sliced

1 medium onion, peeled and diced

3 cloves garlic, peeled and minced

¼ teaspoon ground black pepper

1 (12-ounce) package Garden City All Natural Lavash Whole Wheat Roll-Ups

1 cup shredded Swiss cheese

1 small jalapeño pepper, seeded and sliced

2 tablespoons chopped fresh cilantro

¼ cup nonfat sour cream

1 Heat oil in a medium skillet over medium heat. Add mushrooms, onion, and garlic and cook, stirring, until brown and tender, about 10 minutes. Sprinkle with black pepper.

2 Heat a large nonstick skillet or griddle over medium-low heat. Place a single lavash on the surface, flipping once or twice to warm, then sprinkle ½ cup cheese, half of the jalapeño slices, and 1 tablespoon cilantro evenly over the top.

3 Wait 2–3 minutes for cheese to melt, then spread with half of the mushroom mixture. Sandwich with a second lavash, then carefully flip the entire quesadilla over to toast on the second side. Cook until second side is slightly crisp, about 2 minutes.

4 Remove from griddle and place on a clean, flat surface. Using a pizza cutter or sharp knife, slice quesadilla into 8 wedges.

5 Repeat process with the remaining ingredients.

6 Serve hot, garnished with nonfat sour cream.

Salt-Free-tos

SERVES 6

Per Serving:

Calories	130
Fat	5g
Sodium	8mg
Carbohydrates	17g
Fiber	2g
Sugar	2g
Protein	1g

RECIPE NOTES

Although fried, only a fraction of the oil in this recipe is absorbed into the chips; the rest drains off onto paper towels. Nutritional yeast, such as Red Star, is sold at health food stores and some supermarkets, often with the baking products, seasonings, or bulk foods. Its salty, cheese-like taste adds a tremendous low-sodium boost to many foods.

Lip-smacking, finger-licking good, and completely salt-free! These homemade seasoned tortilla chips are just like your old favorites, but better. Benson's Salt-Free Seasonings are sold online at www.bensonsgourmetseasonings.com.

3 tablespoons nutritional yeast flakes

1½ tablespoons Benson's Table Tasty Salt Substitute

1 tablespoon Benson's Salt-Free Bravado Seasoning

10 (5") corn tortillas

1 cup canola oil

1 Measure nutritional yeast, salt substitute, and seasoning into a small paper bag. Close securely and shake to combine. Set aside.

2 Stack tortillas, 3 or 4 at a time, and cut into 6 equal-sized wedges using a pizza cutter or sharp knife. Repeat the process with all tortillas until you have a total of 60 wedges, or chips.

3 Line a large baking sheet with paper towels and set aside.

4 Heat oil in a large skillet over medium heat. Add several tortilla wedges to the skillet, being careful not to overcrowd. The chips cook quickly and have a tendency to stick together. Cook until crisp and golden, about 30 seconds, then remove from skillet and place on paper towels to drain. If chips begin to brown too quickly, reduce heat.

5 Place chips in the paper bag with the nutritional yeast mixture. Close securely and shake to coat. Remove chips from bag and place on a wire rack to cool.

6 Repeat the process until all chips are cooked and seasoned.

7 Serve immediately or store in an airtight container until serving.

Seasoned Sesame Kale Chips

Light as air, crisp, and addictive, these chips get their salty taste from low-sodium kale seasoning. Another salt-free seasoning may be substituted if you prefer.

1 bunch fresh kale

2½ teaspoons Bragg Organic Sea Kelp Delight Seasoning

2 teaspoons toasted sesame seeds

1 Preheat oven to 325°F. Lightly spray a baking sheet with nonstick cooking spray and set aside.

2 Wash kale and pat dry. Remove leaves from the tough stalks, cut or tear into pieces, and arrange in a single layer on the prepared baking sheet (two batches may be needed if kale doesn't fit on one sheet).

3 Spray kale lightly with nonstick cooking spray and sprinkle with seasoning and sesame seeds.

4 Place baking sheet on middle rack in oven and bake 12 minutes. Remove from oven and transfer chips to a sheet of wax paper or foil to cool. Repeat process with the remaining ingredients.

5 Store in an airtight container.

SERVES 4

Per Serving:

Calories	41
Fat	1g
Sodium	77mg
Carbohydrates	7g
Fiber	2g
Sugar	0g
Protein	2g

WHAT IS KELP?

Kelp is a type of harvested seaweed. It's naturally low in sodium with a pronounced salty taste, making it an excellent salt substitute. Kelp is low in fat and calories, aids metabolism through its high concentration of iodine, and is a great source of vitamin K and folate. Kelp is sold in dried form, either alone or as part of a seasoning blend. Maine Coast Sea Seasonings Organic Kelp Granules and Bragg Organic Sea Kelp Delight Seasoning are two such products; both are sold in select stores and online.

Sweet Potato Crisps

SERVES 2	
Per Serving:	
Calories	93
Fat	4g
Sodium	21mg
Carbohydrates	12g
Fiber	2g
Sugar	4g
Protein	1g

Love store-bought sweet potato chips? This homemade version is so good you may never buy them again. Adapted from www .chowhound.com.

1 medium sweet potato, peeled
2 teaspoons olive oil
½ teaspoon ground paprika

1. Position two oven racks in the middle of the oven. Preheat oven to 350°F.
2. Slice the sweet potato into paper-thin rounds using a mandoline or very sharp knife.
3. Place slices in a medium bowl, add oil and paprika, and toss to coat. Arrange slices in a single layer on two large baking sheets. Do not overlap.
4. Place baking sheets on middle two racks in oven and bake 8 minutes. Switch the baking sheet positions and bake another 7–8 minutes, until the edges of the slices begin to curl and the centers are golden brown and dry to the touch.
5. Remove baking sheets from oven and place on wire racks. Cool for a few minutes before transferring to a bowl. Serve immediately or store in an airtight container for up to 3 days.

Chewy Granola Bars

These soft and chewy granola bars make a healthy, fat-free change from their commercial counterparts. They're perfect for a quick energy boost or a guilt-free go-to snack anytime. Adapted from WomenHeart's All Heart Family Cookbook.

3 cups quick oats

1 cup white whole-wheat flour

2 teaspoons sodium-free baking soda

1 teaspoon ground cinnamon

¼ teaspoon ground nutmeg

1½ cups unsweetened applesauce

¾ cup light brown sugar

2 teaspoons vanilla extract

⅔ cup raisins or dried cranberries

1 Preheat oven to 350°F. Spray two 8" square baking pans lightly with nonstick cooking spray and set aside.

2 Place oats, flour, baking soda, cinnamon, and nutmeg in a large bowl and whisk to combine.

3 Add applesauce, brown sugar, and vanilla and mix. Stir in raisins (or cranberries). Divide the mixture evenly between the two prepared pans and smooth the tops with a spatula. Place pans on the middle rack in oven and bake 20 minutes.

4 Remove pans from oven and place on a wire rack to cool briefly. Cut each pan into 10 equal-sized bars. Carefully remove bars from pans and place on wire rack to cool. Serve immediately, store in an airtight container, or wrap individually and freeze.

SERVES 20

Per Serving:

Calories	122
Fat	1g
Sodium	4mg
Carbohydrates	27g
Fiber	2g
Sugar	13g
Protein	2g

DIFFERENCES IN OATS

Oats come in three main types. Quick or instant oats have been precooked and dried. They have the fastest cooking time and are great for making oatmeal or adding to baked goods. Old-fashioned rolled oats have been put through a steaming process to speed cooking. They're considered all-purpose and work well in most recipes. Steel-cut oats, sometimes labeled "Scotch" or "Irish," are cut, not rolled. They have a chewy texture that's good for oatmeal and other recipes, but because of their longer cooking time, aren't ideal for everything.

Homemade Soft Pretzels

Delicious, hot-from-the-oven soft pretzels are easier to make than you'd think. After baking, spray them lightly with nonstick cooking spray or olive oil and sprinkle them with your choice of seasoning. Enjoy the pretzels plain or serve them with salt-free mustard.

4½ teaspoons dry active yeast

1½ cups warm water

2 tablespoons honey

3 cups unbleached all-purpose flour

1 cup white whole-wheat flour

1 large egg, beaten

SERVES 10	
Per Serving:	
Calories	200
Fat	1g
Sodium	8mg
Carbohydrates	41g
Fiber	3g
Sugar	4g
Protein	6g

1 Preheat oven to 425°F.

2 Place yeast in a large bowl. Add water, honey, and flours and stir to combine. Turn dough out onto a lightly floured surface and knead 5 minutes.

3 Divide dough into 10 equal pieces. Roll each piece into a long snake-like tube, then twist to form a pretzel. Place pretzels on a large baking sheet and brush lightly with the beaten egg.

4 Place baking sheet on middle rack in oven and bake 15 minutes until golden brown. Remove from oven and place pretzels on a wire rack to cool.

Whole-Grain Crackers with Rosemary, Garlic, and Parmesan

Per Serving (6 crackers):	
Calories	95
Fat	4g
Sodium	38mg
Carbohydrates	12g
Fiber	2g
Sugar	1g
Protein	3g

PARMESAN CHEESE

Parmesan cheese can add a lot of flavor, but it can also add unwanted fat and sodium. When selecting a cheese, check nutrition facts carefully. BelGioioso Grated Parmesan is one of the lowest in both fat and sodium, containing only 1 gram of fat per tablespoon and a mere 45 milligrams of sodium. BelGioioso is sold in many supermarkets and specialty cheese shops.

These crisp crackers make super snacks. Partner them with soup, sliced Swiss cheese, and crunchy grapes for a wonderful light meal.

1⅔ cups white whole-wheat flour

½ teaspoon sodium-free baking powder

1 tablespoon salt-free all-purpose seasoning

1 teaspoon ground rosemary

1 teaspoon garlic powder

½ cup low-fat milk

¼ cup grated Parmesan cheese

3 tablespoons olive oil

1 large egg white

1 Preheat oven to 400°F. Spray a baking sheet lightly with nonstick cooking spray and set aside.

2 Place flour, baking powder, seasoning, rosemary, and garlic powder in a medium bowl and whisk to combine.

3 Add milk, cheese, oil, and egg white and stir to make a stiff dough. Add 1–2 tablespoons of water if the dough is too dry.

4 Turn the dough out onto a lightly floured surface and knead several minutes, until dough is smooth and intact. Roll out to about ⅛" thick.

5 Cut into 1½" squares and transfer to the prepared baking sheet.

6 Place baking sheet on middle rack in oven and bake 10 minutes. Remove from oven and place crackers on a wire rack to cool. Store in an airtight container.

CHAPTER 4

Dips, Condiments, Marinades, and Sauces

Basil Pesto

GROW YOUR OWN

Fresh herbs are easy and inexpensive to grow in almost any living situation. A sunny windowsill or patio planter can produce enough to flavor a wide array of recipes for months to come. A few bargain pots, some soil, and seeds are all you need to get started. Whichever herbs you like best, enjoy them conveniently and at their freshest by growing your own.

Stir a little bit of this fragrant pesto into pasta or rice for a taste sensation, or use it as a spread for sandwiches or a topping for pizza.

2 cups fresh basil leaves

4 cloves garlic, peeled

3 tablespoons olive oil

¼ cup pine nuts

2 tablespoons grated Parmesan cheese

¼ teaspoon ground black pepper

1 Place all ingredients in a food processor and pulse until smooth.
2 Use immediately or store in an airtight container and refrigerate until use.

Cilantro Peanut Pesto

A flavorful change from standard basil pesto, this zesty Asian-inspired sauce is great on grains, pasta, and more.

½ cup fresh cilantro leaves

¼ cup light coconut milk

¼ cup unsalted peanuts

4 cloves garlic, peeled

2 tablespoons lime juice

1 tablespoon grated lime zest

1 Place all the ingredients in a food processor and pulse until smooth.

2 Use immediately or store in an airtight container and refrigerate until use.

MAKES ½ CUP	
Per Serving (2 tablespoons):	
Calories	79
Fat	5g
Sodium	5mg
Carbohydrates	6g
Fiber	1g
Sugar	2g
Protein	2g

Sour Cream and Onion Dip

MAKES 1 CUP

Per Serving (1 tablespoon):

Calories	23
Fat	0g
Sodium	42mg
Carbohydrates	4g
Fiber	0g
Sugar	0g
Protein	1g

This rich, creamy, and guilt-free alternative to commercial dips makes a terrific topping for baked potatoes, a stir-in for scrambled eggs, and partner for freshly cut vegetables.

1 medium onion, peeled and diced

1 cup nonfat sour cream

1 teaspoon salt-free all-purpose seasoning

¼ teaspoon garlic powder

1 Spray a medium skillet with nonstick cooking spray and heat over medium heat. Sauté onion until soft and brown, 3–5 minutes.

2 Place the remaining ingredients in a small bowl. Add sautéed onion and stir to combine.

3 Cover and refrigerate at least 2 hours before serving.

Holy Guacamole

Vibrant in color and flavor, this simple dip makes any meal more special. Serve it with everything from chips to tacos to rice and beans. Guacamole is best consumed fresh, so serve it the same day you make it.

1 large avocado, peeled, pitted, and diced

1 small tomato, chopped

2 tablespoons lime juice

2 cloves garlic, peeled and minced

1 tablespoon chopped fresh cilantro

½ teaspoon ground cumin

⅛ teaspoon ground cayenne pepper

1 Place avocado in a deep bowl and mash with a fork, as smoothly or coarsely as desired.

2 Stir in the remaining ingredients.

3 Serve immediately or cover and refrigerate 1 hour before serving.

MAKES 1 CUP	
Per Serving (2 tablespoons):	
Calories	45
Fat	3g
Sodium	3mg
Carbohydrates	3g
Fiber	2g
Sugar	0g
Protein	0g

AVOCADO FACTS

Avocados are native to South and Central America and are actually a fruit, not a vegetable. Ripe avocados have a smooth, leathery skin that when ripe yields gently to pressure. The easiest way to prepare a ripe avocado is to cut lengthwise through the fruit to the core, gently break open, remove the pit, and peel away the skin. Avocados are high in vitamins B_6, C, E, and K, and have been shown to protect against prostate cancer.

Roasted Red Pepper Hummus

Flavored by succulent roasted pepper, this colorful dip is great with chips or vegetables, and it also makes a wonderful low-sodium sandwich spread.

MAKES 1½ CUPS

**Per Serving
(2 tablespoons):**

Calories	79
Fat	2g
Sodium	6mg
Carbohydrates	12g
Fiber	3g
Sugar	2g
Protein	3g

1 (15-ounce) can no-salt-added chickpeas, drained and rinsed

⅓ cup chopped Roasted Red Peppers (see recipe in Chapter 11)

2 cloves garlic, peeled

2 tablespoons lemon juice

2 tablespoons sesame tahini

1 Place all ingredients in a food processor and pulse until smooth.

2 Serve immediately or cover and refrigerate until serving.

Garlic Lovers Hummus

Hummus is the ultimate vegetarian dip and sandwich filling. This version calls for tahini, a smooth sesame butter sold in many supermarkets and natural food stores. If you can't find it, try substituting low-sodium vegetable broth. For a milder flavor, reduce the amount of garlic.

1 (15-ounce) can no-salt-added chickpeas, drained and rinsed

3 tablespoons sesame tahini

3 tablespoons lemon juice

2 tablespoons olive oil

4 cloves garlic, peeled

1 Place all ingredients in a food processor and pulse until smooth.

2 Serve immediately or cover and refrigerate at least 1 hour before serving.

MAKES 1½ CUPS

Per Serving (2 tablespoons):

Calories	103
Fat	5g
Sodium	7mg
Carbohydrates	11g
Fiber	3g
Sugar	2g
Protein	4g

Pineapple Salsa

**Per Serving
(2 tablespoons):**

Calories	14
Fat	0g
Sodium	1mg
Carbohydrates	4g
Fiber	0g
Sugar	2g
Protein	0g

Fresh, ripe fruits make the best salsas, and juicy pineapple is among the best. Add an extra jalapeño or two for fire.

½ medium pineapple, peeled, cored, and finely diced

1 small jalapeño pepper, seeded and minced

1 small red bell pepper, seeded and diced

3 cloves garlic, peeled and minced

2 tablespoons lime juice

¼ cup chopped fresh cilantro

1. Place all ingredients in a medium bowl and stir to combine.
2. Serve immediately or cover and refrigerate until ready to serve.

Orange Cranberry Sauce

**Per Serving
(2 tablespoons):**

Calories	66
Fat	0g
Sodium	1mg
Carbohydrates	17g
Fiber	1g
Sugar	15g
Protein	0g

This thick relish makes a superb low-sodium sandwich topping, a wonderful addition to breakfast, or a fantastic garnish for roasted meat.

1 cup orange juice

1 cup sugar

3 cups whole cranberries

1 medium clementine, peeled, segmented, and coarsely chopped

1 Place juice and sugar in a small stockpot and stir to combine. Bring to a boil over high heat.

2 Add cranberries and clementine, reduce heat to medium, and simmer for 10 minutes.

3 Remove from heat and cover. Allow to cool to room temperature before serving.

Spicy Lime, Cilantro, and Garlic Marinade

This marinade provides the most amazing citrusy, garlicky, spicy southwestern taste imaginable. Toss meat or tofu in the marinade and refrigerate it for at least 1 hour. Thanks to Tammy and Sarita for sharing!

2 teaspoons olive oil

½ cup finely chopped fresh cilantro

4 cloves garlic, peeled and minced

1 tablespoon dried red pepper flakes

¼ cup lime juice

Combine all ingredients in a small bowl and whisk to combine. Use immediately or cover and refrigerate for up to 1 week.

MAKES 1 CUP	
Per Serving (¼ cup):	
Calories	28
Fat	2g
Sodium	1mg
Carbohydrates	2g
Fiber	0g
Sugar	0g
Protein	0g

Mango Salsa

MAKES 2 CUPS

Per Serving
(2 tablespoons):

Calories	16
Fat	0g
Sodium	1mg
Carbohydrates	4g
Fiber	0g
Sugar	3g
Protein	0g

Ripe mangoes, garlic, lime, and cilantro flavor this mouth-wateringly tasty salsa.

1 medium mango, peeled, pitted, and diced

1 small red bell pepper, seeded and chopped

2 cloves garlic, peeled and minced

1 small jalapeño pepper, seeded and minced

2 tablespoons lime juice

2 tablespoons chopped fresh cilantro

1 tablespoon apple cider vinegar

1 teaspoon agave nectar

1 teaspoon ground cumin

1 Place all ingredients in a medium bowl and stir to combine.

2 Serve immediately or cover and refrigerate until ready to serve.

Roasted Tomato Salsa

This delicious, flavorful salsa with roasted tomato, pepper, and onion is fairly mild; to increase the heat, leave the jalapeño seeds in or add additional hot peppers.

5 medium tomatoes

1 medium green bell pepper

1 medium onion

3 cloves garlic, peeled and minced

1 small jalapeño pepper, seeded and minced

1 tablespoon chopped fresh cilantro

3 tablespoons apple cider vinegar

1 teaspoon ground cumin

⅛ teaspoon liquid smoke

MAKES 2 CUPS	
Per Serving (2 tablespoons):	
Calories	11
Fat	0g
Sodium	3mg
Carbohydrates	2g
Fiber	<1g
Sugar	1g
Protein	0g

1. Preheat oven to 450°F. Spray a baking sheet lightly with nonstick cooking spray.

2. Slice tomatoes in half and place cut-side down on the prepared baking sheet. Slice bell pepper in half, remove core and seeds, and place cut-side down on baking sheet. Peel and trim onion, slice in half, and place cut-side down on baking sheet. Place pan on middle rack in oven and roast for 15 minutes.

3. Remove baking sheet from oven and let rest until cool enough to touch. Gently peel skins from tomatoes and bell pepper. Lift tomatoes from baking sheet (they will be very soft) and gently squeeze out and discard seeds. Transfer tomato pulp to a medium bowl.

4. Chop roasted bell pepper and onion and add to bowl.

5. Add garlic, jalapeño, cilantro, vinegar, cumin, and liquid smoke to the bowl and stir to combine.

6. Serve immediately or cover and refrigerate until ready to serve.

Faux Soy Sauce

MOLASSES ALERT!

When making Faux Soy Sauce and other dishes, look for the lowest-sodium molasses you can find. Grandma's Original Unsulphured Molasses and Crosby's Fancy Molasses are both very low in sodium. If you can't locate either, check labels carefully before purchase. Some molasses brands contain high levels of sodium; it's better to be safe than sorry.

Meet soy sauce's tasty cousin, Faux. Pair it with other Asian ingredients, and you'll never know the difference. Adapted from Dick Logue's Soy Sauce Substitute.

¼ **cup molasses**

3 **tablespoons unflavored rice wine vinegar**

1 **tablespoon water**

1 **teaspoon sodium-free beef bouillon granules**

½ **teaspoon ground black pepper**

1 Place all ingredients in a small saucepan and heat on low to combine, about 1 minute. Or heat in microwave in a small microwave-safe bowl.

2 Use immediately or store in an airtight container and refrigerate until ready to use.

Asian-Inspired Low-Sodium Marinade

Adapted from Cooking Light *magazine, this low-sodium marinade has subtle nuances of garlic and ginger, 5-spice powder, and the sweet tang of rice wine vinegar. Marinate your choice of meat for at least 2 hours, turning occasionally, before grilling or broiling.*

3 tablespoons Faux Soy Sauce (see recipe in this chapter)

1½ tablespoons honey

1 tablespoon unflavored rice wine vinegar

1½ teaspoons canola oil

2 cloves garlic, peeled and minced

1½ tablespoons grated fresh ginger

¼ teaspoon 5-spice powder

¼ teaspoon ground black pepper

1 Combine all ingredients in a small bowl.
2 Use immediately or store in an airtight container and refrigerate until ready to use.

MAKES ½ CUP	
Per Serving (1 tablespoon):	
Calories	32
Fat	1g
Sodium	2mg
Carbohydrates	6g
Fiber	0g
Sugar	5g
Protein	0g

Salt-Free Mayonnaise

MAKES 1 CUP

Per Serving (1 tablespoon):

Calories	84
Fat	9g
Sodium	7mg
Carbohydrates	0g
Fiber	0g
Sugar	0g
Protein	0g

LIQUID EGG SUBSTITUTES

Sold in cartons beside the eggs, liquid egg substitutes such as Egg Beaters are a great way of enjoying the flavor of whole eggs without the fat and cholesterol. Substitute ¼ cup of liquid egg substitute for each egg in most recipes without a discernable difference in taste or texture. Liquid egg substitutes can be frozen as well, making them both healthy and convenient.

Adapted from Southern Living *magazine, this light and creamy mayonnaise uses liquid egg substitute, eliminating cholesterol and the risk of salmonella.*

¼ cup liquid egg substitute (e.g., Egg Beaters)
2½ tablespoons distilled white vinegar
½ teaspoon ground white pepper
⅛ teaspoon garlic powder
⅛ teaspoon ground mustard
⅛ teaspoon ground cayenne pepper
⅔ cup canola oil

1 Place egg substitute, vinegar, white pepper, garlic powder, mustard, and cayenne in a food processor and pulse until smooth. Scrape down sides.
2 With food processor running, add the oil in a slow and steady stream until thickened.
3 Use immediately or store in an airtight container and refrigerate until ready to use (and keep refrigerated when not in use).

Spicy, Sweet, and Tangy Barbecue Sauce

Salt-free, fat-free, and absolutely amazing, this authentic-tasting barbecue sauce is perfect for all your grilling, basting, and dipping needs.

2 (8-ounce) cans no-salt-added tomato sauce

3 tablespoons apple cider vinegar

2 tablespoons molasses

1 tablespoon honey

1 teaspoon liquid smoke

2 teaspoons onion powder

1½ teaspoons ground cumin

1 teaspoon ground paprika

½ teaspoon garlic powder

½ teaspoon ground black pepper

⅛ teaspoon ground cayenne pepper

1 Combine all ingredients in a small saucepan and simmer over medium-low heat for 10 minutes.

2 Remove from heat and pour into a clean lidded jar. Refrigerate until ready to use.

MAKES 2 CUPS

Per Serving (2 tablespoons):

Calories	24
Fat	0g
Sodium	4mg
Carbohydrates	5g
Fiber	0g
Sugar	4g
Protein	0g

Salt-Free Ketchup

MAKES 3 CUPS

Per Serving (1 tablespoon):

Calories	9
Fat	0g
Sodium	3mg
Carbohydrates	2g
Fiber	0g
Sugar	1g
Protein	0g

TIPS TO REDUCE DIETARY SODIUM

Seek out products that are labeled "salt free" or "no salt added." Canned goods such as tomatoes, vegetables, and beans all come in salt-free varieties. And don't forget the condiments! Salt-free versions of ketchup, mustard, and even pickles, are all available in supermarkets and online. Salt-free products will save you hundreds of milligrams of sodium per serving.

No need to purchase commercial salt-free ketchup when it's this easy to make at home. It contains no artificial additives, preservatives, or sweeteners—and it's delicious!

3 (8-ounce) cans no-salt-added tomato sauce
5 tablespoons no-salt-added tomato paste
3 tablespoons distilled white vinegar
5 teaspoons sugar
¼ teaspoon garlic powder
¼ teaspoon onion powder
⅛ teaspoon ground mustard
⅛ teaspoon ground cinnamon
⅛ teaspoon ground cumin

1 Place all ingredients in a 3-quart saucepan and stir until completely smooth.
2 Place pan over medium heat. As soon as mixture begins to bubble, reduce heat to low and simmer for 10 minutes.
3 Remove from heat and pour ketchup into a clean lidded jar. Refrigerate when not using.

Salt-Free Chili Seasoning

If you have difficulty finding commercial salt-free chili seasoning at the grocery store, make your own! It's quick and affordable, and the ingredients can be adjusted to suit your taste.

2 tablespoons ground cumin

1 tablespoon ground coriander

2 teaspoons dried oregano

1½ teaspoons ground paprika

½ teaspoon dried red pepper flakes

½ teaspoon garlic powder

½ teaspoon onion powder

¼ teaspoon ground mustard

⅛ teaspoon ground cayenne pepper

1 Place all ingredients in a small bowl and whisk to combine.
2 Store seasoning in a small lidded jar.

MAKES ⅓ CUP	
Per Serving (¼ teaspoon):	
Calories	0
Fat	0g
Sodium	0mg
Carbohydrates	0g
Fiber	0g
Sugar	0g
Protein	0g

Salt-Free Italian Seasoning

MAKES ⅓ CUP

Per Serving (¼ teaspoon):

Calories	0
Fat	0g
Sodium	0mg
Carbohydrates	0g
Fiber	0g
Sugar	0g
Protein	0g

PRESERVING DRIED HERBS AND SPICES

Many people position their spice rack close to the stove for easy access during cooking. But the proximity to heat and humidity compromises flavor and longevity. To maximize freshness, store dried herbs and spices in a cool, dark cabinet away from direct sunlight and cooking.

This dried-herb blend is great for pasta dishes, pizzas, and other Italian foods.

2 tablespoons dried basil

1 tablespoon dried oregano

2 teaspoons dried rosemary

1½ teaspoons dried thyme

1 teaspoon dried marjoram

½ teaspoon ground sage

1 Place all ingredients in a small bowl and whisk to combine.

2 Store seasoning in a small lidded jar.

CHAPTER 5

Salads and Dressings

Edamame Salad with Corn and Cranberries

Try this delightfully chewy, crisp, and colorful salad to brighten plates and palates year-round.

1¼ cups shelled edamame

¾ cup fresh or frozen corn kernels

1 small red or orange bell pepper, seeded and diced

¼ cup dried cranberries

1 small shallot, peeled and finely diced

2 tablespoons red wine vinegar

1 tablespoon olive oil

1 teaspoon agave nectar

1 teaspoon no-salt-added prepared mustard

¼ teaspoon ground black pepper

SERVES 4	
Per Serving:	
Calories	149
Fat	5g
Sodium	5mg
Carbohydrates	22g
Fiber	3g
Sugar	10g
Protein	5g

1 Place edamame, corn, bell pepper, cranberries, and shallot in a medium bowl and stir to combine.

2 In a small bowl, whisk together vinegar, oil, agave nectar, and mustard.

3 Pour the dressing over the salad and toss to coat. Season with black pepper.

4 Serve immediately or cover and refrigerate until ready to serve.

Tangy Three-Bean Salad with Barley

SERVES 8

Per Serving:

Calories	367
Fat	11g
Sodium	10mg
Carbohydrates	57g
Fiber	11g
Sugar	11g
Protein	11g

BRAGG APPLE CIDER VINEGAR

A wonderful low-sodium product, Bragg Apple Cider Vinegar is organic, raw, and unfiltered. The brownish cobweb-like residue that collects on the bottom of each bottle, known as the "Mother," contains amazing health properties, similar to the live active cultures in yogurt. Use Bragg just as you would distilled apple cider vinegar, and enjoy the added nutrition it bestows. Bragg is sold in many supermarkets and natural food stores.

If you prefer your green beans more tender, steam for a few minutes before adding to the salad. Many thanks to Janelle for sharing!

1 cup pearled barley

2¼ cups water

2 cups fresh green beans, trimmed and cut into 2" pieces

1 (15-ounce) can no-salt-added kidney beans, drained and rinsed

1 (15-ounce) can no-salt-added chickpeas, drained and rinsed

1 medium red bell pepper, seeded and diced

1 small onion, peeled and finely chopped

2 tablespoons chopped fresh cilantro or parsley

⅓ cup canola oil

⅓ cup apple cider vinegar

⅓ cup maple syrup

¼ teaspoon ground black pepper

1 Place barley and water in a medium saucepan and bring to a boil over high heat. Reduce heat to low, cover, and simmer until water is absorbed, 25–30 minutes. Drain barley in a colander and rinse with cool water. Transfer to a large bowl.

2 Add green beans, kidney beans, chickpeas, bell pepper, onion, and cilantro (or parsley) to the bowl and stir to combine.

3 In a small bowl, whisk together oil, vinegar, and maple syrup. Pour over the salad and toss to coat. Season with black pepper.

4 Cover and refrigerate at least 4 hours before serving.

Fresh Corn, Pepper, and Avocado Salad

The next time you make corn on the cob, set aside a few ears for this fabulous summer salad.

3 large ears fresh corn, cooked

1 medium red bell pepper, seeded and diced

1 medium avocado, peeled, pitted, and diced

1 small jalapeño pepper, seeded and minced

1 scallion, thinly sliced

1 clove garlic, peeled and minced

2 tablespoons lime juice

2 tablespoons olive oil

¼ teaspoon ground black pepper

1 Cut the kernels from the corn carefully, using a very sharp knife. Place in a large bowl. Add bell pepper, avocado, jalapeño, scallion, and garlic.

2 In a small bowl, whisk together lime juice and oil. Drizzle over salad and toss to coat. Season with black pepper.

3 Serve immediately or cover and refrigerate until ready to serve.

SERVES 6

Per Serving:

Calories	135
Fat	9g
Sodium	5mg
Carbohydrates	13g
Fiber	3g
Sugar	2g
Protein	2g

CORN FACTS

Corn is high in vitamin C, is a great source of both protein and fiber, and contains antioxidants associated with reduced risk of cardiovascular disease and hypertension. It can be eaten hot or cold, on the cob or in single kernels, and even popped. Corn grows easily in the home garden. Its sweet taste and vibrant color adds flavor, interest, and added nutrition to any meal.

Garlic Potato Salad

SERVES 6

Per Serving:

Calories	204
Fat	9g
Sodium	6mg
Carbohydrates	28g
Fiber	2g
Sugar	1g
Protein	2g

GARLIC SCAPES

Long tendrils with a small bulb at one end, garlic scapes may look like something you'd simply toss into the compost, but they're a real showstopper in terms of taste. Garlic scapes are milder in flavor than their clove counterparts and can be eaten raw, minced finely, or sliced like green beans. If you've never seen or used them before, head to a summer farmers' market and pick up some.

This toothsome concoction of potatoes, scallions, and garlic is hefty enough to fill you up, yet light enough to be refreshing. You can make it with garlic scapes or the more readily available clove garlic. Either way, this deliciously simple salad is a showcase of flavor. Adapted from Simply in Season.

6 medium potatoes

6 garlic scapes or 3 cloves garlic, peeled and chopped

1 cup sliced scallions

¼ cup olive oil

2 tablespoons unflavored rice vinegar

2 teaspoons chopped fresh rosemary

¼ teaspoon ground black pepper

1 Put potatoes in a large saucepan and add enough water to cover by 1". Place over high heat and bring to a boil. Boil until fork-tender but still solid, depending upon size, 20–25 minutes.

2 Remove from heat and place under cold running water. Drain and set potatoes aside to cool for 15 minutes. Cut into cubes and place in a large bowl.

3 Add garlic and scallions and toss to combine.

4 In a small bowl, whisk together oil, vinegar, rosemary, and pepper. Pour dressing over salad and stir gently to coat. Cover and refrigerate at least 3 hours before serving.

Southwestern Beet Slaw

This simple salad will make a beet lover out of you! Shredded beets are combined with carrots, scallions, garlic, cilantro, and a lime vinaigrette. The resulting salad is subtly sweet, spicy, and spectacular.

3 medium beets, trimmed, peeled, and shredded

3 scallions, sliced

2 medium carrots, peeled and shredded

¼ cup chopped fresh cilantro

2 cloves garlic, peeled and minced

3 tablespoons lime juice

1 teaspoon olive oil

½ teaspoon salt-free chili seasoning

¼ teaspoon ground black pepper

1 Place beets in a large bowl. Add scallions, carrots, cilantro, and garlic and stir to combine.

2 In a small bowl, whisk together lime juice, oil, chili seasoning, and pepper. Pour dressing over beet mixture and toss to coat.

3 Serve immediately or cover and refrigerate at least 2 hours before serving.

SERVES 6

Per Serving:

Calories	38
Fat	1g
Sodium	46mg
Carbohydrates	7g
Fiber	2g
Sugar	4g
Protein	1g

Salade Niçoise

SERVES 2

Per Serving:

Calories	471
Fat	20g
Sodium	111mg
Carbohydrates	41g
Fiber	7g
Sugar	5g
Protein	30g

The famous French salad is re-created in a low-sodium style. Delightful and impressive, it's a plate full of color, flavor, and protein with a dreamy dressing that pulls it all together.

2 medium red potatoes

1 tablespoon distilled white vinegar

2 large eggs

1 pound green beans, trimmed

2 tablespoons olive oil

2 tablespoons red wine vinegar

1 teaspoon no-salt-added prepared mustard

1 clove garlic, peeled and minced

½ teaspoon ground black pepper

1 small head butter lettuce, torn into bite-sized pieces

1 small cucumber, peeled, seeded, and sliced

2 small tomatoes, quartered

1 (5-ounce) can no-salt-added tuna in water, drained

1. Place potatoes in a medium saucepan and add enough water to cover. Bring to a boil over high heat. Reduce heat to medium-low and simmer until tender, about 20 minutes. Drain potatoes and transfer them to a cutting board. Dice potatoes and place in a large bowl. Add white vinegar and toss to coat. Set aside.

2. Place eggs in a small saucepan, add enough water to cover, and bring to a boil over high heat. Boil 12 minutes. Drain and cool in a bowl of cold water for 5 minutes. Carefully crack, peel, and slice eggs into quarters. Set aside.

3. Bring a small saucepan of water to a boil over high heat. Add green beans and cook for 2 minutes. Remove beans from the pan and immediately place in a bowl of ice water. Set aside.

4. In a small bowl, whisk together oil, red wine vinegar, mustard, garlic, and pepper.

5. Assemble the salad on a platter, placing lettuce on the bottom and then grouping cucumber, potatoes, eggs, green beans, tomatoes, and tuna on top. Drizzle dressing evenly over salad. Serve immediately.

Warm Kale Salad

SERVES 4	
Per Serving:	
Calories	137
Fat	3g
Sodium	76mg
Carbohydrates	25g
Fiber	4g
Sugar	7g
Protein	5g

Warm and filling, with a citrus sweetness and red pepper kick, this salad makes a great side dish or light meal.

2 teaspoons olive oil

1 small red onion, peeled and diced

2 cloves garlic, peeled and minced

1 small red bell pepper, seeded and diced

8 cups chopped kale

¼ cup fresh orange juice

1 medium carrot, peeled and shredded

¼ teaspoon ground cumin

⅛ teaspoon dried red pepper flakes

1 teaspoon grated orange zest

¼ teaspoon ground black pepper

1 Heat oil in a large skillet over medium heat. Add onion and sauté for 2 minutes.
2 Add garlic, bell pepper, kale, and orange juice and stir to combine. Reduce heat to medium-low, cover, and cook for 5 minutes.
3 Remove lid and stir in carrot, cumin, red pepper flakes, orange zest, and black pepper. Cover and cook for another 5 minutes.
4 Remove from heat and serve immediately.

Tabbouleh Salad

This refreshing low-sodium salad is a wonderful way to start any meal. For a party, set out tabbouleh with sliced fresh vegetables and a bowl of homemade hummus.

⅔ cup couscous

1 cup boiling water

1 small tomato, diced

1 small green bell pepper, seeded and diced

1 small shallot, peeled and finely diced

⅓ cup chopped fresh parsley

1 clove garlic, peeled and minced

3 tablespoons lemon juice

1 tablespoon olive oil

½ teaspoon ground black pepper

1 Place couscous in a small bowl. Stir in boiling water, cover, and set aside for 5 minutes.

2 Place tomato, bell pepper, shallot, and parsley in a salad bowl. Add couscous and stir to combine.

3 In a small bowl, whisk together garlic, lemon juice, oil, and black pepper. Pour dressing over the couscous mixture and toss to coat.

4 Serve immediately or cover and refrigerate until ready to serve.

SERVES 4	
Per Serving:	
Calories	120
Fat	3g
Sodium	6mg
Carbohydrates	20g
Fiber	1g
Sugar	1g
Protein	3g

PARSLEY FACTS

Parsley is an easy-to-grow herb that comes in two varieties: flat-leaf and curly. Too often it's dismissed as a bland plate garnish, but parsley has amazing, distinctive flavor when eaten raw. Use it to add refreshing taste and color to salads, dressings, and pastas. Parsley contains high levels of vitamins A, C, and K as well as antioxidants, and may help prevent cardiovascular disease.

Tart Apple Salad with Fennel and Honey Yogurt Dressing

SERVES 6

Per Serving:

Calories	70
Fat	<1g
Sodium	26mg
Carbohydrates	16g
Fiber	3g
Sugar	11g
Protein	1g

FENNEL FACTS

Fennel is a vegetable with a pronounced anise (black licorice) flavor and aroma. Every part of the plant is edible and can be eaten either raw or cooked. Fennel has a firm white bulb from which green celery-like stalks grow, ending in soft, dill-like fronds. When it blossoms, its flowers produce small, edible, anise-flavored seeds. Fennel is high in fiber and protein, is said to alleviate stomach upset and gas, and contains antioxidants linked to preventing heart disease and cancer.

The fennel really makes this salad and can be used in its entirety—bulb, stalks, and fronds. Leave the peel on the apples for added nutrients and fiber.

2 medium green apples, cored and diced

1 small bulb fennel, trimmed and chopped

1½ cups seedless red grape halves

2 tablespoons lemon juice

¼ cup low-fat vanilla yogurt

1 teaspoon honey

1 Combine all ingredients in a medium bowl and stir.
2 Serve immediately or cover and refrigerate until ready to serve.

Thai Pasta Salad

Colorful fresh vegetables and the flavors of sesame and ginger make this hearty pasta salad a treat. Serve it warm or cold.

1 (16-ounce) package spaghetti

2 tablespoons plus ⅓ cup peanut oil, divided

1 medium yellow squash, trimmed and julienned

1 medium zucchini, trimmed and julienned

1 medium green bell pepper, seeded and julienned

1 medium red bell pepper, seeded and julienned

1 medium orange bell pepper, seeded and julienned

6 scallions, sliced

3 cloves garlic, peeled and minced

1 small jalapeño pepper, seeded and minced

¾ cup chopped walnuts

1 tablespoon sesame oil

¼ cup unflavored rice vinegar

2 tablespoons salt-free peanut butter

1 tablespoon no-salt-added tomato paste

¼ cup chopped fresh cilantro

1 tablespoon minced fresh ginger

1 teaspoon sugar

¼ teaspoon salt-free chili seasoning

SERVES 8	
Per Serving:	
Calories	464
Fat	24g
Sodium	9mg
Carbohydrates	50g
Fiber	5g
Sugar	4g
Protein	11g

1 Bring a large pot of water to a boil over high heat. Break spaghetti in half and add to the pot. Cook for 10 minutes, stirring once or twice. Remove from heat, drain, and set aside.

2 Heat 2 tablespoons peanut oil in a large skillet over medium heat. Add julienned vegetables, scallions, garlic, jalapeño, and walnuts and cook, stirring, for 3–4 minutes.

3 Remove from heat and transfer to a very large bowl. Add cooked spaghetti.

4 Whisk together remaining ⅓ cup peanut oil, sesame oil, vinegar, peanut butter, tomato paste, cilantro, ginger, sugar, and chili seasoning in a small bowl. Pour over pasta salad and toss to coat. Serve immediately or cover and refrigerate until ready to serve.

Whole-Wheat Couscous Salad with Citrus and Cilantro

SERVES 6

Per Serving:

Calories	126
Fat	2g
Sodium	5mg
Carbohydrates	24g
Fiber	2g
Sugar	3g
Protein	4g

WHAT IS COUSCOUS?

Couscous is a tiny grain-like pasta made from semolina (wheat) flour. It cooks in minutes and makes an easy and convenient alternative to rice and other grains. Couscous comes in white and whole-wheat varieties; the whole-wheat version has the added benefits of whole grain, thus making it a healthier choice. Couscous is low in fat and sodium and is a good source of protein, fiber, and iron. It's sold in most supermarkets and natural food stores, both in packages and dry bulk bins, and is often stocked alongside rice and other grains.

This whole-grain salad strikes the perfect balance between light and filling. Its refreshing taste can be enjoyed year-round, but is best in summer with produce picked fresh from the garden.

1½ cups water

1 cup whole-wheat couscous

1 medium cucumber, peeled, seeded, and sliced

1 pint grape or cherry tomatoes, halved

1 small jalapeño pepper, seeded and minced

2 small shallots, peeled and minced

2 scallions, sliced

2 cloves garlic, peeled and minced

2 tablespoons lemon juice

2 tablespoons lime juice

1 teaspoon olive oil

¼ cup chopped fresh cilantro

¼ teaspoon ground black pepper

1 Bring water to a boil over high heat in a medium saucepan. Stir in couscous, reduce heat to medium-low, cover, and simmer for 2 minutes. Remove pan from heat, uncover, and fluff couscous with a fork. Set aside to cool for 5 minutes.

2 Transfer couscous to a large bowl and add the remaining ingredients. Stir to combine.

3 Serve immediately or cover and refrigerate until ready to serve.

Simple Autumn Salad

This healthy and delicious salad is a tasty combination of red leaf lettuce, red onion, fruit, and walnuts in a light and tangy vinaigrette.

1 large head red leaf lettuce, torn into bite-sized pieces

1 medium pear, cored and thinly sliced

½ small red onion, peeled and thinly sliced

½ cup chopped dried figs

⅓ cup chopped walnuts

2 tablespoons white balsamic vinegar

2 tablespoons olive oil

1 clove garlic, peeled and minced

¼ teaspoon ground black pepper

1 Place lettuce, pear, onion, figs, and walnuts in a large bowl.

2 In a small bowl, whisk together vinegar, oil, garlic, and pepper. Pour dressing over salad and toss to coat. Serve immediately.

SERVES 4	
Per Serving:	
Calories	224
Fat	14g
Sodium	29mg
Carbohydrates	25g
Fiber	5g
Sugar	15g
Protein	3g

STOCK UP AND SAVE

There's nothing more irritating than running out of a crucial ingredient when you're ready to cook. And this goes doubly when you're following a specialized diet and don't have the luxury of ordering out. By buying items in bulk, you'll not only be saving money, as per-unit costs are often less expensive, but you'll also be hedging against future inconvenience.

Arugula with Pears and Red Wine Vinaigrette

The peppery taste of arugula is paired with crisp, sweet pears and a tangy red wine vinaigrette. Add grilled chicken, dried figs, and/or shredded cheese for a main-course salad.

8 cups fresh baby arugula

2 medium pears, cored and thinly sliced

¼ cup chopped pecans

4 tablespoons red wine vinegar

2 tablespoons olive oil

1 clove garlic, peeled and minced

½ teaspoon dried marjoram

¼ teaspoon ground mustard

¼ teaspoon ground black pepper

SERVES 4	
Per Serving:	
Calories	137
Fat	9g
Sodium	13mg
Carbohydrates	15g
Fiber	3g
Sugar	9g
Protein	2g

1 Place arugula, pears, and pecans in a large bowl.

2 In a small bowl, whisk together vinegar, oil, garlic, marjoram, mustard, and pepper. Pour over salad and toss to coat. Serve immediately.

Tuna Pasta Salad with Broccoli and Sun-Dried Tomatoes

HOW IS VINEGAR MADE?

Vinegar is produced when an alcoholic liquid is allowed to ferment and the ethanol within it oxidizes. The remaining liquid becomes highly acidic, and is what we refer to as *vinegar*. Balsamic vinegar is made from the leftover pressings, or must, of white grapes that are first boiled down to form a syrup, then allowed to age. Apple cider vinegar is made from a similar process using apple must.

Bold flavors combine flawlessly in this healthy salad. With whole grains, low-fat protein, vitamins, and nutrients, it's a one-dish meal that's wonderful served warm or cold.

½ cup chopped sun-dried tomatoes (not in oil)

1 cup boiling water

1 (13-ounce) package whole-grain penne

1 tablespoon olive oil

1 large head broccoli, cut into small florets

2 small shallots, peeled and finely diced

2 (5-ounce) cans no-salt-added tuna in water, drained

2 tablespoons balsamic vinegar

½ teaspoon ground black pepper

1 Place sun-dried tomatoes in a medium bowl, add water, and let soak for 10 minutes. Drain, reserving 2 tablespoons of the soaking liquid.

2 Cook penne according to package directions, omitting salt. Drain and set aside.

3 Heat oil in a large skillet over medium-high heat. Add broccoli and sauté for 5 minutes. Remove from heat. Add sun-dried tomatoes, reserved soaking liquid, penne, shallots, tuna, vinegar, and pepper to the skillet and stir to combine.

4 Serve immediately or cover and refrigerate until ready to serve.

Strawberry Vinaigrette

This dressing is sweet with a smidgen of tart acidity and so much flavor. It's a colorful complement to any salad ingredients, from greens to fruit. But don't stop there. Try it with grilled meat or even drizzled over cake! Adapted from Simply in Season.

1 cup sliced fresh strawberries

4 teaspoons unseasoned rice vinegar

4 teaspoons lemon juice

1 tablespoon sugar

1½ teaspoons honey

⅛ teaspoon garlic powder

⅛ teaspoon onion powder

⅛ teaspoon dried basil

⅛ teaspoon ground black pepper

4 tablespoons olive oil

1 Place strawberries in a blender or food processor and pulse until smooth. Add vinegar, lemon juice, sugar, honey, garlic powder, onion powder, basil, and pepper and blend until combined.
2 Gradually add oil and pulse until combined.
3 Use immediately or store in an airtight container and refrigerate. Use within 2 days.

MAKES 1½ CUPS

**Per Serving
(2 tablespoons):**

Calories	53
Fat	4g
Sodium	0mg
Carbohydrates	3g
Fiber	0g
Sugar	2g
Protein	0g

BEHIND THE SCENES OF HONEY PRODUCTION

Honey is a liquid sweetener made when honeybees consume nectar and bring it back to their hive. As the bees transport the nectar from flower to hive, it mixes with special enzymes in their saliva, forming honey. Although this may sound less than appealing, honey is anything but. Apart from its amazing taste, raw honey is said to help heal wounds and infections, protect against allergies, and even inhibit disease.

Lemon Vinaigrette

Get ready to lick your plate! This irresistibly zesty dressing adds sparkle to salads and makes a great marinade for vegetables, meat, and tofu.

MAKES 3 OUNCES	
Per Serving (1 ounce):	
Calories	69
Fat	4g
Sodium	0mg
Carbohydrates	8g
Fiber	0g
Sugar	6g
Protein	0g

¼ cup lemon juice

1 tablespoon olive oil

1 tablespoon minced shallot

1 tablespoon honey

⅛ teaspoon ground white pepper

1 Place all ingredients in a small bowl and whisk to combine.

2 Use immediately or cover and refrigerate until ready to serve.

Apple Honey Mustard Vinaigrette

Toss this tart, tangy, absolutely delicious dressing with salad greens or use it as a sauce for sautéed spinach, Swiss chard, or kale.

MAKES ½ CUP	
Per Serving (2 tablespoons):	
Calories	65
Fat	3g
Sodium	1mg
Carbohydrates	9g
Fiber	0g
Sugar	8g
Protein	0g

¼ cup apple cider vinegar

2 tablespoons honey

1 tablespoon olive oil

1 teaspoon ground mustard

⅛ teaspoon ground white pepper

1 Place all ingredients in a small bowl and whisk to combine.

2 Use immediately or cover and refrigerate until ready to serve.

Italian Vinaigrette

This simple, all-purpose salad dressing also works well as a marinade.

3 tablespoons distilled white vinegar

1½ teaspoons olive oil

2 cloves garlic, peeled and minced

½ teaspoon salt-free Italian seasoning

½ teaspoon salt-free all-purpose seasoning

1 Place all ingredients in a small bowl and whisk to combine.

2 Use immediately or cover and refrigerate until ready to serve.

MAKES ¼ CUP	
Per Serving (2 tablespoons):	
Calories	37
Fat	3g
Sodium	1mg
Carbohydrates	1g
Fiber	0g
Sugar	0g
Protein	0g

Sesame Ginger Vinaigrette

Modeled after the dressings served at many Japanese restaurants, this low-sodium vinaigrette will have you craving salads like never before.

¼ cup unflavored rice wine vinegar

1 tablespoon sesame oil

1 tablespoon minced fresh ginger

2 cloves garlic, peeled and minced

1 teaspoon sugar

¼ teaspoon ground white pepper

1 Place all ingredients in a small microwave-safe bowl and whisk to combine.

2 Microwave for 30 seconds and whisk again. Pour over salad and toss to coat. Serve immediately.

MAKES ⅓ CUP	
Per Serving (2 tablespoons):	
Calories	58
Fat	5g
Sodium	0mg
Carbohydrates	2g
Fiber	0g
Sugar	1g
Protein	0g

Vegan Caesar Salad Dressing

MAKES ¼ CUP

**Per Serving
(2 tablespoons):**

Calories	106
Fat	10g
Sodium	10mg
Carbohydrates	4g
Fiber	1g
Sugar	0g
Protein	3g

OWN YOUR OWN HEALTH

Transitioning to a healthy diet often requires dramatic changes in thought and behavior. A good way to encourage yourself is to leave reminders around the house. Tape small notes to the outside and inside of the refrigerator, for example, reminding you of the importance of healthy choices. It's easy to lose sight of these things, especially when you're hungry.

With undertones of garlic and lemon, this smooth and creamy dressing provides all the flavor of the classic Caesar without the cholesterol. Toss it with crisp romaine lettuce and Salt-Free Croutons (see recipe in Chapter 11) or serve it as a dip with raw vegetables.

¼ **cup pine nuts or chopped walnuts**
¼ **cup low-sodium vegetable broth**
2 **cloves garlic, peeled**
1 **tablespoon lemon juice**
¼ **teaspoon ground mustard**
⅛ **teaspoon ground white pepper**

1　Place all ingredients in a food processor and pulse until smooth.
2　Serve immediately.

CHAPTER 6
Soups, Stews, and Chilis

Apple Butternut Soup

SERVES 6

Per Serving:

Calories	150
Fat	0g
Sodium	8mg
Carbohydrates	38g
Fiber	1g
Sugar	11g
Protein	3g

APPLE FACTS

Apples are one of the most widely consumed fruits in the world. They can be eaten raw, cooked, dried, juiced, or fermented, without diminishing their nutritional value. For best health, buy organic apples, wash, and consume along with the skin. The peel provides added nutrients and fiber. Apples contain vitamins C and K as well as flavonoids, substances believed to prevent cancer.

Apples draw out the natural sweetness of butternut squash, delivering a smooth, irresistibly delicious fat-free soup.

6 cups diced butternut squash

2 cups diced apple

6 cups water

2 cups unsweetened apple juice

½ teaspoon ground cinnamon

⅛ teaspoon ground allspice

1 Place squash, apple, water, and apple juice in a large stockpot and bring to a boil over high heat. Reduce heat to medium-low, cover, and simmer for 20 minutes.

2 Remove pot from heat and transfer contents to a blender or food processor. Purée until smooth.

3 Return soup to the pot, add cinnamon and allspice, and stir to combine. Serve warm.

Easy Wonton Soup

This low-sodium soup is so similar to classic wonton soup, you'll be hard-pressed to tell the difference. Add your choice of fresh mushrooms, from basic white button or baby bella to oyster or shitake.

½ pound lean ground pork

1 tablespoon minced fresh ginger

4 cloves garlic, peeled and minced

8 cups low-sodium chicken broth

2 cups sliced fresh mushrooms

6 ounces whole-grain yolk-free egg noodles

¼ teaspoon ground white pepper

4 scallions, sliced

1 Place a large stockpot over medium heat. Add ground pork, ginger, and garlic and sauté for 5 minutes. Drain any excess fat, then return to stovetop over medium heat.
2 Add broth and bring to a boil. Stir in mushrooms, noodles, and pepper. Cover and simmer for 10 minutes.
3 Remove pot from heat. Stir in scallions and serve immediately.

SERVES 8	
Per Serving:	
Calories	143
Fat	4g
Sodium	90mg
Carbohydrates	14g
Fiber	1g
Sugar	1g
Protein	12g

Banana Coconut Soup with Tropical Fruit

This sublime soup offers a taste of paradise in mere minutes. Serve it as a cool starter, a light dessert, or a lovely addition to breakfast.

SERVES 4	
Per Serving:	
Calories	235
Fat	7g
Sodium	24mg
Carbohydrates	42g
Fiber	4g
Sugar	31g
Protein	1g

2 medium bananas, peeled

1 (14-ounce) can light coconut milk

1 tablespoon honey

⅛ teaspoon ground cardamom

1 medium mango, peeled, pitted, and diced

1 medium kiwi, peeled and sliced

2 cups cubed fresh pineapple

1 Place bananas and coconut milk in a food processor and purée.

2 Pour contents of food processor into a medium bowl. Add honey and cardamom and stir to combine.

3 Divide evenly between four bowls, then top with fruit. Serve immediately.

Carrot Soup with Ginger

Bursting with vitamin A, this low-fat soup gets an A+ for its delightful taste and fabulous color.

CARROT FACTS

Vibrant, crunchy, and sweetly delicious, carrots are a beloved vegetable among humans and animals alike. They can be eaten raw, cooked, or juiced. Carrots contain high levels of vitamin A and antioxidants, and are believed to help prevent cancer.

4 cups diced carrot

1 cup diced sweet potato

1 cup diced sweet onion

4 cups low-sodium vegetable or chicken broth

1 tablespoon minced fresh ginger

2 tablespoons chopped fresh parsley

1 Combine carrot, sweet potato, onion, broth, and ginger in a medium saucepan and bring to a boil over high heat. Reduce heat to low and simmer, covered, for 30 minutes.

2 Remove from heat and purée using a blender or food processor. Serve immediately, garnished with parsley.

Black Bean Vegetable Soup

Thick and hearty, with a deep, rich taste, this vegetarian soup is ready in less than 30 minutes. Don't drain the canned tomatoes or beans; the liquid becomes part of the flavorful stock.

1 small red onion, peeled and diced

3 cloves garlic, peeled and minced

2½ cups low-sodium vegetable broth, divided

1 small carrot, peeled and diced

1 stalk celery, diced

1 small sweet potato, peeled and diced

1 (15-ounce) can no-salt-added diced tomatoes

1 (15-ounce) can no-salt-added black beans

¼ cup red wine

1 tablespoon no-salt-added tomato paste

1½ teaspoons ground cumin

1 teaspoon dried oregano

½ teaspoon ground coriander

¼ teaspoon dried red pepper flakes

¼ teaspoon ground black pepper

2 tablespoons chopped fresh cilantro

SERVES 4	
Per Serving:	
Calories	233
Fat	2g
Sodium	88mg
Carbohydrates	41g
Fiber	8g
Sugar	6g
Protein	10g

1 Place a medium stockpot over medium heat. Add onion, garlic, and ¼ cup broth and sauté for 2 minutes.

2 Add another ¼ cup broth, carrot, celery, sweet potato, and tomatoes with juice and sauté for 3 minutes.

3 Add remaining 2 cups broth, beans, wine, tomato paste, cumin, oregano, coriander, red pepper flakes, and black pepper. Bring to a boil, cover, and simmer for 15–20 minutes until vegetables are tender.

4 Remove from heat, stir in cilantro, and serve immediately.

Basic Low-Sodium Broth

MAKES 8 CUPS

Per Serving (1 cup):

Calories	12
Fat	0g
Sodium	9mg
Carbohydrates	3g
Fiber	0g
Sugar	2g
Protein	0g

HOMEMADE VERSUS COMMERCIAL BROTH

Homemade broth is often tastier than store-bought, and it's also additive- and preservative-free. Homemade broth can be made in batches and frozen for later use. When pressed for time, however, commercial low-sodium broths can be a good alternative, as long as they're also low in fat. Check nutrition facts carefully; some manufacturers sell "reduced-sodium" broths that contain hundreds of milligrams per serving. Some excellent commercial broths are made by Pacific Foods, Imagine Foods, and Kitchen Basics.

This fat-free vegan broth is perfect for flavoring your favorite soup or sipping straight from a mug.

1 medium yellow onion, peeled and quartered

3 cloves garlic, peeled and halved

8 ounces button mushrooms, roughly chopped

3 medium carrots, peeled and cut into chunks

2 stalks celery, cut into chunks

2 medium tomatoes, roughly chopped

1 (1") piece fresh ginger, peeled

6 whole peppercorns

2 bay leaves

10 cups water

1 Place all ingredients in a large stockpot.

2 Cover pot and bring to a boil over high heat. Reduce heat to medium-low and simmer for 30 minutes.

3 Turn off the heat and let the contents steep for another 30 minutes.

4 Pour broth through a fine-mesh sieve, discarding solids. Use immediately, store in the refrigerator for up to a week, or freeze.

Cheesy Potato Chowder

This creamy, dreamy concoction of potatoes, chicken broth, and cheese will make a low-sodium soup fan of anyone.

1 tablespoon olive oil

2 cups diced onion

1 cup diced celery

2 cloves garlic, peeled and minced

6 cups diced potato

4 cups low-sodium chicken broth

⅓ cup dry white wine

½ teaspoon dried thyme

¼ teaspoon ground rosemary

¼ teaspoon dried basil

¼ teaspoon ground black pepper

1 cup shredded Swiss cheese

SERVES 6	
Per Serving:	
Calories	252
Fat	8g
Sodium	94mg
Carbohydrates	33g
Fiber	3g
Sugar	3g
Protein	11g

1 Heat oil in a large stockpot over medium heat. Add onion, celery, and garlic and sauté for 5 minutes. Add potato and cook, stirring, for 1 minute. Add broth, wine, thyme, rosemary, basil, and pepper. Bring to a boil.

2 Reduce heat to low, cover, and simmer for 20 minutes.

3 Remove pot from heat. Using a blender or food processor, purée half the soup. Return to pot and stir to combine.

4 Add cheese and stir until melted. Serve hot.

Chicken Soup with Jalapeño and Lime

SERVES 8

Per Serving:

Calories	118
Fat	2g
Sodium	111mg
Carbohydrates	9g
Fiber	1g
Sugar	3g
Protein	6g

HOT, HOT, HOT!

Hot peppers, or chili peppers, add tremendous dimension to food without upping the sodium ante. Hot peppers come in many colorful varieties and vary widely in heat, from the fairly mild jalapeño to the nearly intolerable Scotch bonnet. Hot peppers are easy to grow in the garden, and can be preserved through freezing or drying. To freeze, simply seal in an airtight container and freeze for up to a year. To dry peppers, place on a flat surface until they shrivel and dehydrate, or string them and hang to dry.

Set your taste buds abuzz with the zing of fresh lime! This low-sodium, low-fat soup is brimming with flavor. For added heft, ladle the soup over bowls of cooked brown or wild rice.

2 cups shredded cooked chicken

1 medium red onion, peeled and diced

3 cloves garlic, peeled and minced

2 medium carrots, peeled and sliced

1 stalk celery, sliced

1 medium red bell pepper, seeded and diced

1 small jalapeño pepper, seeded and minced

1 (15-ounce) can no-salt-added diced tomatoes

¼ cup lime juice

8 cups low-sodium chicken broth

1 teaspoon ground cumin

½ teaspoon ground coriander

¼ teaspoon dried oregano

½ teaspoon ground black pepper

2 tablespoons chopped fresh cilantro

1 medium lime, cut into wedges

1 Place chicken, onion, garlic, carrots, celery, bell pepper, jalapeño, tomatoes, lime juice, broth, cumin, coriander, oregano, and black pepper in a large stockpot and bring to a boil over high heat.

2 Reduce heat to low, cover, and simmer for 15 minutes.

3 Remove from heat, ladle into bowls, and garnish with cilantro and lime wedges. Serve immediately.

Garden Tomato Soup

Ripe tomatoes, sweet bell pepper, and onion partner perfectly in this fresh vegetable soup. Serve it with grilled Swiss cheese sandwiches for a sensational low-sodium meal.

1 tablespoon olive oil

3 cups chopped and seeded tomatoes

1 cup chopped onion

1 cup chopped red bell pepper

1 tablespoon minced garlic

4 cups low-sodium vegetable broth

2 tablespoons no-salt-added tomato paste

1 tablespoon chopped fresh basil

1 teaspoon chopped fresh oregano

½ teaspoon chopped fresh thyme

¼ teaspoon ground black pepper

1 Heat oil in a medium stockpot over medium heat. Add tomatoes, onion, bell pepper, and garlic and cook, stirring, for 10 minutes.

2 Add broth, tomato paste, basil, oregano, thyme, and black pepper and stir to combine. Raise heat to high and bring to a boil.

3 Reduce heat to low, cover, and simmer for 10 minutes.

4 Remove from heat and purée using a blender or food processor. Serve immediately.

SERVES 4

Per Serving:

Calories	130
Fat	5g
Sodium	20mg
Carbohydrates	19g
Fiber	2g
Sugar	4g
Protein	3g

TIPS TO REDUCE DIETARY SODIUM

Use fresh, local, organic produce whenever possible. Fresh fruits and vegetables have not been processed, meaning nothing has been added to them, including salt. By buying organic produce, you protect yourself from the risks associated with harmful chemical pesticides and fertilizers. And by supporting local farmers, you ensure their livelihood and the continuation of the food stock you enjoy.

Classic Chicken Noodle Soup

No cookbook would be complete without this perennial favorite. This low-fat, low-sodium version makes the most of meaty chicken and tender vegetables.

2 cups shredded cooked chicken

2 medium carrots, peeled and sliced

1 stalk celery, sliced

1 small onion, peeled and diced

3 cloves garlic, peeled and minced

4 cups low-sodium chicken broth

1 teaspoon salt-free all-purpose seasoning

½ teaspoon ground sage

¼ teaspoon ground rosemary

¼ teaspoon ground black pepper

1½ cups yolkless egg noodles

SERVES 4	
Per Serving:	
Calories	291
Fat	5g
Sodium	167mg
Carbohydrates	26g
Fiber	2g
Sugar	2g
Protein	33g

1 Combine chicken, carrots, celery, onion, garlic, broth, seasoning, sage, rosemary, and pepper in a medium stockpot. Bring to a boil over high heat.

2 Add noodles, reduce heat to medium-low, and simmer for 10 minutes.

3 Remove from heat. Ladle soup into bowls and serve immediately.

Kale Soup with Lemon and Tuna

CANNED TUNA CONCERN

Studies show that many brand-name tunas often exceed the FDA's advisory limits for mercury and should not be consumed with regularity. If you are buying supermarket tuna, opt for chunk light over white albacore, as the light tuna is lower in mercury. Some premium tuna brands, such as Oregon's Choice, contain far lower levels of mercury and higher values of omega-3s. Oregon's Choice Gourmet No Salt Added Albacore Tuna can be purchased online.

The citrus kiss of this healthy soup brings sunshine to the darkest days. No-salt-added canned tuna adds protein and omega-3 fatty acids. Substitute another cooked fish if you like or omit it for a strictly vegetarian soup.

1 teaspoon olive oil

1 large shallot, peeled and minced

3 cloves garlic, peeled and minced

6 tablespoons lemon juice

8 cups chopped fresh kale

4 cups low-sodium chicken or vegetable broth

2 (5-ounce) cans no-salt-added tuna in water

¼ cup wheat berries

1 teaspoon dried herbes de Provence

¼ teaspoon ground black pepper

1 Heat oil in a medium stockpot over medium heat. Add shallot and garlic and sauté for 2 minutes. Add lemon juice and kale and cook, stirring, until kale has wilted, about 2 minutes.

2 Add broth, tuna, wheat berries, herbes de Provence, and pepper and cover. Increase heat to high and bring to a boil. Reduce heat to low and simmer for 20 minutes.

3 Remove from heat and serve immediately.

Red Lentil Soup with Bacon

Filled with vegetables, this low-fat lentil soup has a light, delicious broth enhanced by the smoky flavor of low-sodium bacon. Red lentils are used here because of their smaller size and shorter cooking time. If you want to substitute brown lentils, increase the simmering time to 40 minutes.

2 slices low-sodium bacon, diced

1 medium onion, peeled and diced

3 cloves garlic, peeled and minced

2 medium carrots, peeled and diced

2 stalks celery, diced

2 cups dried red lentils, rinsed

8 cups low-sodium beef broth

2 bay leaves

½ teaspoon dried savory

½ teaspoon dried thyme

¼ teaspoon dried basil

¼ teaspoon dried oregano

⅛ teaspoon dried red pepper flakes

¼ teaspoon ground black pepper

1 Place a large stockpot over medium heat. Add bacon, onion, and garlic and sauté for 5 minutes. Add carrots and celery and sauté for 2 minutes.

2 Add lentils, broth, bay leaves, savory, thyme, basil, oregano, red pepper flakes, and black pepper and stir to combine. Increase heat to high and bring to a boil.

3 Reduce heat to low, cover pot, and simmer, stirring occasionally, until lentils are tender, 20–30 minutes.

4 Remove from heat, remove bay leaves, and serve.

SERVES 8	
Per Serving:	
Calories	175
Fat	2g
Sodium	114mg
Carbohydrates	25g
Fiber	8g
Sugar	3g
Protein	14g

Mushroom Soup with Orzo

SERVES 6

Per Serving:

Calories	138
Fat	3g
Sodium	75mg
Carbohydrates	21g
Fiber	2g
Sugar	3g
Protein	10g

WHAT IS ORZO?

Orzo is a small, oval-shaped pasta, with an appearance similar to rice. It's made from semolina flour, a type of wheat flour, making it an unacceptable choice for those with celiac disease. For a gluten-free alternative, try substituting cooked brown rice.

A warming dish for a nippy day, this soup is filled with the earthy flavors of mushrooms and garlic.

24 ounces fresh mushrooms

1 teaspoon olive oil

1 medium onion, peeled and diced

1 stalk celery, diced

6 cloves garlic, peeled and minced

6 cups low-sodium chicken or vegetable broth

½ teaspoon dried rosemary, crumbled

½ teaspoon dried sage, crumbled

½ teaspoon dried thyme

¼ teaspoon ground black pepper

⅔ cup orzo pasta

1. Slice half of the mushrooms, chop the rest, and set aside.
2. Heat oil in a medium stockpot over medium heat. Add onion, celery, and garlic and sauté for 3 minutes. Add mushrooms and cook, stirring, for 7 minutes.
3. Add broth, rosemary, sage, thyme, and pepper and raise heat to high, bringing to a boil.
4. Reduce heat to low and stir in orzo. Cover the pot and simmer 20 minutes.
5. Remove from heat and serve.

Sweet Potato and Chickpea Soup

The intoxicating aromas of India were the inspiration for this sensational soup. Serve it garnished with chopped fresh cilantro.

1 teaspoon olive oil

1 large shallot, peeled and chopped

1 clove garlic, peeled and minced

1 (1") piece fresh ginger, peeled and minced

1 teaspoon salt-free garam masala

½ teaspoon ground paprika

⅛ teaspoon dried red pepper flakes

4 cups low-sodium chicken or vegetable broth

4 cups cubed sweet potato

½ cup sliced carrot

1 (15-ounce) can no-salt-added chickpeas, drained and rinsed

2 tablespoons chopped fresh cilantro

SERVES 4	
Per Serving:	
Calories	348
Fat	5g
Sodium	163mg
Carbohydrates	60g
Fiber	10g
Sugar	18g
Protein	16g

1 Heat oil in a medium stockpot over medium heat. Add shallot and garlic and sauté for 2 minutes. Add ginger, garam masala, paprika, and red pepper flakes and cook, stirring, for 30 seconds.

2 Add broth and stir to combine. Stir in sweet potatoes, carrots, and chickpeas.

3 Increase heat to high and bring to a boil. Cover the pot, reduce heat to medium-low, and simmer for 15 minutes, stirring occasionally.

4 Remove from heat. Ladle into bowls, garnish with cilantro, and serve immediately.

Summer Vegetable Stew

SERVES 6

Per Serving:

Calories	122
Fat	2g
Sodium	16mg
Carbohydrates	17g
Fiber	3g
Sugar	9g
Protein	2g

FRESH VERSUS DRIED

When adding flavor to uncooked foods such as salads or salsas, fresh herbs are often best. Some herbs, such as parsley and cilantro, don't retain the level of flavor when dried, and their textures suffer too. When adding herbs to foods that will be cooked or simmered for a length of time, dried herbs may be a better choice. Many dried herbs have a more concentrated flavor than their fresh counterparts and stand up well to cooking. When substituting between the two, use three times the fresh herbs for dried, or 1 tablespoon fresh herb for every 1 teaspoon dried.

This flavorful dish is light enough for the hottest of days, yet hearty enough to satisfy. Pair it with Soft and Crusty No-Rise Rolls (see recipe in Chapter 11) for a lovely meal. Salt-free canned tomatoes may be substituted for fresh when making this out of season.

2 teaspoons olive oil
1 medium onion, peeled and diced
4 cloves garlic, peeled and minced
1 small/medium eggplant, peeled and diced
2 small yellow squash, trimmed and diced
2 small zucchini, trimmed and diced
6 small tomatoes, diced
2 (8-ounce) cans no-salt-added tomato sauce
1 cup red wine
1 teaspoon dried basil
1 teaspoon dried marjoram
¾ teaspoon ground black pepper
½ teaspoon dried oregano
¼ teaspoon dried savory

1. Heat oil in a large stockpot over medium heat. Add onion and garlic and sauté for 2 minutes. Add eggplant, yellow squash, zucchini, and tomatoes and cook, stirring, for 10 minutes.
2. Add tomato sauce, wine, basil, marjoram, pepper, oregano, and savory and stir to combine.
3. Cover pot and simmer for 20 minutes, stirring occasionally. Serve warm or at room temperature.

Manhattan-Style Seafood Stew

This intoxicating tomato-based stew is filled with the earthy richness of carrots, potatoes, onion, and garlic; the scent of the sea; a touch of citrus; and the kick of cilantro and spicy hot pepper. One bite and you'll agree: It's a salt-free synergy far greater than the sum of its parts. Serve it plain or spoon it over rice or couscous. Adapted from Prevention's Low-Fat, Low-Cost Freezer Cookbook.

SERVES 6	
Per Serving:	
Calories	163
Fat	2g
Sodium	169mg
Carbohydrates	22g
Fiber	4g
Sugar	7g
Protein	15g

1½ teaspoons olive oil

1 large onion, peeled and diced

4 cloves garlic, peeled and minced

2 (15-ounce) cans no-salt-added diced tomatoes

2 medium potatoes, peeled and diced

2 cups low-sodium chicken or vegetable broth

2 medium carrots, peeled and sliced

½ pound white-fleshed fish, cut into 1" chunks

1 small jalapeño pepper, seeded and minced

1 large bay leaf

¼ pound small shrimp, peeled and cleaned

⅓ cup chopped fresh cilantro

½ teaspoon grated orange zest

½ teaspoon ground black pepper

1 Heat oil in a medium saucepan over medium heat. Add onion and garlic and cook, stirring, for 3 minutes. Add tomatoes with juice, potatoes, broth, carrots, fish, jalapeño pepper, and bay leaf and stir to combine.

2 Cover the pot and cook, stirring occasionally, for 15 minutes.

3 Stir in shrimp, cilantro, orange zest, and black pepper. Simmer until shrimp are pink, 5 minutes or less, then remove from heat.

4 Carefully remove bay leaf and serve immediately.

Chicken, Corn, and Black Bean Chili

Per Serving:

Calories	309
Fat	4g
Sodium	81mg
Carbohydrates	42g
Fiber	8g
Sugar	6g
Protein	28g

SLOW COOKER MAGIC

Slow cookers take the work out of many meals, and have an almost magical ability to transform the toughest, most inexpensive cuts of meat into tender, succulent feasts. To make this chicken chili in the slow cooker, simply measure ingredients into the appliance, stir to combine, and cover. Set the slow cooker to low and simmer 6–8 hours.

This yummy low-sodium chili is a little different from the standard variety, thanks to the addition of corn, meaty chunks of chicken, and the virtual absence of tomatoes. Serve it with Perfect Corn Bread (see recipe in Chapter 11) for a truly heavenly meal. Recipe adapted from Kitchen Basics Healthy Cooking with Stock.

2 teaspoons olive oil

1 pound boneless, skinless chicken breasts, cut into ½" cubes

1 medium red onion, peeled and diced

3 cloves garlic, peeled and minced

1 medium green bell pepper, seeded and diced

1 medium red bell pepper, seeded and diced

1 (6-ounce) can no-salt-added tomato paste

2 tablespoons salt-free chili powder

1 teaspoon ground cumin

2 cups low-sodium chicken broth

2 (15-ounce) cans no-salt-added black beans, drained and rinsed

2 cups frozen corn kernels

¼ cup chopped fresh cilantro

¼ teaspoon ground black pepper

1. Heat oil in a large stockpot over medium heat. Add chicken and sauté until the outside is no longer pink, 3–5 minutes.
2. Add onion and garlic and sauté for 2 minutes. Add bell peppers and sauté for 2 minutes. Stir in tomato paste, chili powder, cumin, broth, and beans. Increase heat to high and bring to a boil.
3. Reduce heat to medium-low, cover, and simmer for 20 minutes.
4. Stir in corn, cover, and continue cooking for 5 minutes.
5. Remove from heat and stir in cilantro and black pepper. Serve immediately.

Two-Bean Tempeh Chili

SERVES 8

Per Serving:

Calories	326
Fat	4g
Sodium	97mg
Carbohydrates	58g
Fiber	12g
Sugar	13g
Protein	19g

Here's a vegan chili everyone will love! Tempeh adds just the right texture, along with the beans, to make this a year-round crowd-pleaser.

1 (8-ounce) package organic tempeh, cubed

1 medium onion, peeled and diced

3 cloves garlic, peeled and minced

2 (15-ounce) cans no-salt-added diced tomatoes

2 medium carrots, peeled and diced

1 medium bell pepper, seeded and diced

1 small jalapeño pepper, seeded and minced

1 (6-ounce) can no-salt-added tomato paste

3 (8-ounce) cans no-salt-added tomato sauce

1 (15-ounce) can no-salt-added kidney beans, drained and rinsed

1 (15-ounce) can no-salt-added pinto beans, drained and rinsed

2 teaspoons salt-free chili seasoning

1 teaspoon sugar

1¾ cups frozen corn kernels

¼ cup chopped fresh cilantro

¼ teaspoon ground black pepper

1 Place a large stockpot over medium heat. Add tempeh, onion, and garlic and sauté for 3 minutes. Add tomatoes, carrots, bell pepper, and jalapeño and sauté for 5 minutes.

2 Stir in tomato paste, tomato sauce, beans, chili seasoning, and sugar. Bring to a boil.

3 Reduce heat to low, cover, and simmer for 20 minutes, stirring occasionally.

4 Stir in corn kernels and cook just until heated through, about 2 minutes.

5 Remove pot from heat. Stir in cilantro and black pepper. Serve immediately.

CHAPTER 7

Beef and Pork

30-Minute Ground Beef Pizza

This supremely delicious pizza is flavored with lean ground beef and fresh vegetables. If you thought "real" pizza was gone from your life, think again!

SERVES 4	
Per Serving:	
Calories	302
Fat	8g
Sodium	121mg
Carbohydrates	33g
Fiber	5g
Sugar	6g
Protein	23g

1 cup white whole-wheat flour

1 teaspoon salt-free all-purpose seasoning

1 teaspoon salt-free Italian seasoning

½ teaspoon garlic powder

2 large egg whites

⅔ cup low-fat milk

½ pound lean ground beef

1 medium onion, peeled and chopped

½ cup no-salt-added pasta sauce

2 plum tomatoes, sliced

1 cup sliced mushrooms

1 small bell pepper, seeded and diced

3 cloves garlic, peeled and minced

¼ cup chopped fresh basil

¼ cup shredded Swiss cheese

¼ cup nonfat ricotta cheese

1 Preheat oven to 425°F. Grease and flour a 12" nonstick pizza pan and set aside.

2 Place flour, all-purpose seasoning, Italian seasoning, and garlic powder in a medium bowl and whisk to combine. Stir in egg whites and milk. Pour batter into prepared pizza pan and set aside.

3 Heat a large skillet over medium heat. Add ground beef and onion and cook, stirring, for 5 minutes. Remove from heat and carefully drain any excess fat.

4 Spoon mixture evenly over the batter in the pan. Place pan on middle rack in oven and bake for 20 minutes.

5 Remove pan from oven. Spread pasta sauce evenly over pizza. Top with tomatoes, mushrooms, bell pepper, garlic, and basil. Sprinkle Swiss cheese over the pizza, then dollop with ricotta.

6 Return pan to oven and bake for 5 minutes, until cheese has melted.

7 Remove pizza from oven. Gently remove from pan and cut into 8 slices. Serve immediately.

Easy Spaghetti and Meatballs

Who doesn't like spaghetti and meatballs? Here's a simple, delicious, and inexpensive recipe everyone can agree on. As long as you have the ingredients on hand, it's a meal you can whip up anytime. And the meatballs freeze beautifully, too, so feel free to make several batches and stock up for emergencies.

1 pound extra-lean ground beef

1 medium onion, peeled and grated

2 cloves garlic, peeled and minced

1 large egg white, beaten

½ cup salt-free bread crumbs

1 tablespoon grated Parmesan cheese

1 teaspoon dried basil

½ teaspoon dried oregano

½ teaspoon dried thyme

¼ teaspoon ground black pepper

2 tablespoons olive oil

2 cups no-salt-added pasta sauce

1 pound whole-grain spaghetti

SERVES 8	
Per Serving:	
Calories	387
Fat	8g
Sodium	63mg
Carbohydrates	54g
Fiber	4g
Sugar	4g
Protein	23g

LOVE SPAGHETTI? TRY SPAGHETTI SQUASH!

Spaghetti squash is a type of winter squash, with a firm yellow shell and an inner flesh that shreds into pasta-like strands. To cook spaghetti squash, first slice in half lengthwise. Remove the seeds, then place into a microwave-safe bowl. Add ½ cup water, cover, and microwave on high 10–20 minutes, depending upon size. When tender, remove from microwave and shred into strands using a fork.

1 Place ground beef in a large bowl and add onion and garlic. Mix together using a wooden spoon or your hands. Add egg white, bread crumbs, cheese, basil, oregano, thyme, and pepper and mix thoroughly.

2 Pinch off 1–2 tablespoons of the mixture and roll between your palms to achieve a nice globe. Set the meatball aside and repeat with remaining meat mixture, until you have about 24 meatballs.

3 Heat oil in a large skillet over medium heat. Add meatballs and brown on all sides, 3–5 minutes.

4 Add pasta sauce, reduce heat to low, cover, and simmer for 20 minutes, stirring or shaking the pan every so often.

5 Bring a stockpot of water to a boil over high heat. Add spaghetti and cook according to directions on the package, omitting salt.

6 Drain spaghetti and transfer to a large shallow bowl. Pour sauce and meatballs over spaghetti and serve immediately.

Whole-Grain Pasta with Meat Sauce

SERVES 6

Per Serving:

Calories	387
Fat	5g
Sodium	65mg
Carbohydrates	58g
Fiber	9g
Sugar	6g
Protein	27g

Top your favorite whole-grain pasta with this thick, rich, and hearty salt-free sauce. If you prefer more spice, increase the amount of crushed red pepper. If not, eliminate it altogether. Serve the pasta with a green salad for a complete meal.

1 pound whole-grain pasta

1 pound extra-lean ground beef

1 medium onion, peeled and diced

3 cloves garlic, peeled and minced

2 (8-ounce) cans no-salt-added tomato sauce

⅓ cup red wine

1 tablespoon balsamic vinegar

1 teaspoon dried basil

½ teaspoon dried marjoram

½ teaspoon dried oregano

½ teaspoon dried red pepper flakes

½ teaspoon dried thyme

½ teaspoon ground black pepper

1 Cook pasta according to directions on package, omitting salt. Drain and set aside.

2 Place ground beef, onion, and garlic in a medium skillet over medium heat. Cook, stirring, until beef has browned, about 5 minutes.

3 Add the remaining ingredients and stir to combine. Simmer, uncovered, for 10 minutes, stirring occasionally.

4 Remove from heat and spoon over pasta. Serve immediately.

Beef Tacos

This mini fiesta will feed six people—a great excuse to have friends over for margaritas. Serve the tacos with lettuce, tomato, nonfat sour cream, and Holy Guacamole (see recipe in Chapter 4).

1 pound extra-lean ground beef

1 large onion, peeled and chopped

2 cloves garlic, peeled and minced

1 (8-ounce) can no-salt-added tomato sauce

2 teaspoons low-sodium Worcestershire sauce

1 tablespoon molasses

1 tablespoon apple cider vinegar

1 tablespoon ground cumin

1 tablespoon ground paprika

½ teaspoon dried red pepper flakes

¼ teaspoon ground black pepper

1 (12-count) package low-sodium taco shells

¼ cup chopped fresh cilantro

1 Place ground beef, onion, and garlic in a medium skillet over medium heat and cook, stirring, until the beef is browned, 3–5 minutes.

2 Reduce heat to medium-low and add tomato sauce, Worcestershire sauce, molasses, vinegar, cumin, paprika, red pepper flakes, and black pepper. Simmer, stirring frequently, about 10 minutes.

3 Meanwhile, heat taco shells according to package directions. Remove from oven and set aside.

4 Remove skillet from heat. Stir in cilantro, then spoon mixture into taco shells. Serve immediately.

SERVES 6

Per Serving (2 tacos):

Calories	255
Fat	9g
Sodium	79mg
Carbohydrates	23g
Fiber	2g
Sugar	4g
Protein	18g

LOW-SODIUM WORCESTERSHIRE SAUCE

Traditional Worcestershire sauce derives its unique taste from salted fermented anchovies, and often contains as much as 65 milligrams of sodium per teaspoon. Fortunately, there are low-sodium versions sold commercially, both in stores and online. Look for either Lea & Perrins or French's Reduced Sodium Worcestershire Sauce.

Dirty Rice

SERVES 4

Per Serving:

Calories	272
Fat	4g
Sodium	92mg
Carbohydrates	41g
Fiber	4g
Sugar	4g
Protein	16g

The classic Cajun dish is reworked to be much lower in fat and sodium, but not taste. It makes a wonderful one-skillet supper or side dish. Adapted from The Healthy Cook.

½ **pound extra-lean ground beef**

1 **large onion, peeled and diced**

2 **stalks celery, diced**

2 **cloves garlic, peeled and minced**

1 **medium bell pepper, seeded and diced**

1 **teaspoon sodium-free beef bouillon granules**

1 **cup water**

2 **teaspoons low-sodium Worcestershire sauce**

1½ **teaspoons dried thyme**

1 **teaspoon dried basil**

½ **teaspoon dried marjoram**

¼ **teaspoon ground black pepper**

⅛ **teaspoon ground cayenne pepper**

2 **scallions, sliced**

3 **cups cooked long-grain brown rice**

1 Place ground beef, onion, celery, and garlic in a large skillet over medium heat. Cook until the beef is browned, 3–5 minutes.

2 Add bell pepper, bouillon, water, Worcestershire sauce, thyme, basil, marjoram, black pepper, and cayenne pepper and stir to combine.

3 Bring to a boil, then reduce heat to low, cover, and simmer for 20 minutes.

4 Stir in scallions and simmer, uncovered, for 3 minutes.

5 Remove from heat. Add rice and stir to combine. Serve immediately.

Beef with Bok Choy

Bok choy is a small, crunchy Chinese cabbage, with green leaves and squat white celery-like stalks. This recipe combines stir-fried bok choy with leftover grilled steak for a quick and scrumptious meal. Serve it with cooked brown rice.

2 pounds bok choy

2 teaspoons sesame oil

3 cloves garlic, peeled and minced

1 tablespoon minced fresh ginger

1 small red onion, peeled and thinly sliced

1 teaspoon sodium-free beef bouillon granules

½ teaspoon ground white pepper

½ cup water

½ pound grilled steak, cut into thin slices

1. Break the individual stalks of bok choy off at the base, discarding the small central core. Trim each stalk at the base, then cut stalks and greens into 2" pieces.
2. Heat oil in a wok over medium heat. Add garlic, ginger, and onion and cook, stirring, for 30 seconds. Add bok choy and stir-fry for 2 minutes. Stir in bouillon, pepper, and water, then increase heat to high and cook, stirring, for 5–6 minutes.
3. Add steak and heat through. Remove from heat and serve immediately.

SERVES 4

Per Serving:

Calories	195
Fat	10g
Sodium	132mg
Carbohydrates	5g
Fiber	2g
Sugar	2g
Protein	20g

SESAME OIL

The strong fragrance and flavor of sesame oil is often used in Asian cooking, and adds a unique nuance to food without additional sodium. Sesame oil contains 14 grams of fat per tablespoon, 12 grams of which are unsaturated fat, making it an acceptable part of a healthy diet when used in moderation.

Beef with Pea Pods

This beautifully delicious and salt-free take on a Chinese classic, with toothsome beef and crunchy pea pods, is great served with cooked brown rice.

1 tablespoon peanut oil

3 scallions, sliced

2 cloves garlic, peeled and minced

2 teaspoons minced fresh ginger

¾ pound thin beef steak, sliced into ½" × 3" strips

4 cups fresh pea pods, trimmed

3 tablespoons Faux Soy Sauce (see recipe in Chapter 4)

4 cups cooked brown rice

SERVES 4	
Per Serving:	
Calories	466
Fat	11g
Sodium	71mg
Carbohydrates	64g
Fiber	8g
Sugar	12g
Protein	27g

1 Heat oil in a wok over medium heat. Add scallions, garlic, and ginger and stir-fry for 30 seconds. Add beef and stir-fry for 5 minutes, until beef has browned.

2 Add pea pods and Faux Soy Sauce and stir-fry for 3 minutes.

3 Remove from heat. Spoon over cooked rice and serve immediately.

Pressure Cooker Beef Bourguignon

**INSTANT POT®
INSTRUCTIONS**

Press the Sauté button and melt butter in the Instant Pot®. Sauté onions for 5 minutes. Move onions to the side of the pan, add beef, and brown on all sides, about 5 minutes. Press the Cancel button. Add remaining ingredients, close lid, press the Manual button, and set the time for 20 minutes. Let pressure release naturally for 10 minutes, then quick-release any remaining pressure until the float valve drops.

A pressure cooker cuts the cooking time of this traditional French dish by two-thirds, so it's ready in just 30 minutes! The heavenly smell of simmering beef and onions will have you (and your fortunate guests) salivating.

2 tablespoons unsalted butter

3 large onions, peeled and sliced

2 pounds lean beef stew meat, cubed

2 cups water

1½ cups red wine

2 teaspoons sodium-free beef bouillon granules

½ teaspoon dried marjoram

½ teaspoon dried thyme

½ teaspoon ground black pepper

1 pound white mushrooms, sliced

1 Melt butter in a pressure cooker over medium-high heat. Add onions and cook, stirring, for 5 minutes.

2 Move onions to the side of the pan, add beef, and brown on all sides, about 5 minutes.

3 Add the remaining ingredients and stir to combine. Secure the lid on the pressure cooker and set to high. Increase the heat to high and bring the contents to a boil. Once you hear sizzling, reduce heat to medium and cook for 20 minutes.

4 Remove from heat. Allow pressure cooker to depressurize naturally. Serve immediately.

Pressure Cooker Harvest Stew

This hearty low-sodium dish is savory and filling, with an appealing subtle sweetness. Although it looks and tastes impressive, it couldn't be easier; just pop everything into the pressure cooker, and 30 minutes later it's done!

1 tablespoon olive oil

2 pounds lean beef stew meat, cubed

3 medium carrots, peeled and sliced into thick rounds

2 medium green apples, peeled, cored, and cut into chunks

1 large onion, peeled and diced

1 cup fresh cranberries

4 cloves garlic, peeled and minced

2 cups water

2 teaspoons sodium-free beef bouillon granules

1/3 cup unsweetened apple juice

1 teaspoon dried marjoram

1/2 teaspoon dried savory

1/2 teaspoon dried thyme

1/2 teaspoon ground cinnamon

1/2 teaspoon ground rosemary

1/4 teaspoon ground allspice

1/4 teaspoon ground black pepper

1 Heat oil in a pressure cooker over medium-high heat. Add beef and brown on all sides, 3–5 minutes.

2 Add the remaining ingredients to the pot and stir to combine. Secure lid on the pressure cooker. Once pressurized, reduce heat to medium and cook for 20 minutes.

3 Remove pressure cooker from heat and place in a sink under cold running water. Once cooker is depressurized, remove from sink. Serve immediately.

SERVES 6

Per Serving:

Calories	328
Fat	13g
Sodium	105mg
Carbohydrates	16g
Fiber	3g
Sugar	10g
Protein	35g

INSTANT POT® INSTRUCTIONS

Press the Sauté button and heat oil in the Instant Pot®. Brown beef on all sides, 3–5 minutes. Press the Cancel button. Add remaining ingredients, close lid, press the Manual button, and set the time for 20 minutes. Let pressure release naturally for 10 minutes, then quick-release any remaining pressure until the float valve drops.

Cottage Pie with Sweet Potato Crust

SERVES 6

Per Serving:

Calories	236
Fat	8g
Sodium	83mg
Carbohydrates	23g
Fiber	3g
Sugar	10g
Protein	17g

SHEPHERD'S PIE VERSUS COTTAGE PIE

Shepherd's pie is a traditional British dish of ground lamb and vegetables baked beneath a mashed potato crust. Any pie resembling this, but made without lamb or mutton, is referred to as a cottage pie. Cottage pie is most often made with ground beef, but can include any type of meat or nonmeat. Vegetarian versions of both pies are often made with lentils, bulgur, or beans.

If you have a pressure cooker or Instant Pot®, you can steam the sweet potatoes whole in just 5 minutes.

3 large sweet potatoes, peeled, and cut into large chunks

2 tablespoons unsalted butter

2 tablespoons light brown sugar

½ teaspoon ground cinnamon

1 pound extra-lean ground beef

1 medium onion, peeled and diced

3 cloves garlic, peeled and minced

2 medium carrots, peeled and diced

2 stalks celery, diced

⅓ cup red wine

1 tablespoon no-salt-added tomato paste

2 teaspoons sodium-free beef bouillon granules

1 teaspoon dried marjoram

½ teaspoon dried thyme

½ teaspoon ground black pepper

½ teaspoon ground mustard

¼ teaspoon ground rosemary

1 Preheat oven to 425°F. Take out a 2-quart ovenproof casserole dish and set aside.

2 Measure 1 cup water into the bottom of a large saucepan. Place sweet potatoes in a steamer basket and place in pan. Cover pan and place over high heat. Bring to a boil, then reduce heat to medium. Steam sweet potatoes until tender, 15–20 minutes.

3 Drain and mash sweet potatoes. Add butter, brown sugar, and cinnamon and stir to combine. Set aside.

4 Heat a medium skillet over medium heat. Add ground beef, onion, and garlic and cook, stirring, for 5 minutes. Reduce heat to medium; add carrots, celery, wine, tomato paste, bouillon, marjoram, thyme, pepper, mustard, and rosemary and cook, stirring, for 5 minutes. Remove from heat and spoon beef filling into the 2-quart casserole dish.

5 Spoon mashed sweet potatoes over the top and smooth evenly to form a top crust.

6 Place pan on middle rack in oven and bake for 15 minutes. Remove from oven and serve immediately.

Seared Sirloin Steaks with Garlicky Greens

Serve this juicy, medium-rare beef accented with tart and tangy kale with roasted potatoes and fresh corn for a spectacular meal in a snap. Adapted from Fine Cooking.

1½ pounds sirloin steak (1" thick)

1 tablespoon chopped fresh rosemary

¾ teaspoon ground black pepper, divided

1 tablespoon olive oil

¾ cup dry white wine

4 cloves garlic, peeled and minced

2 tablespoons white balsamic vinegar

1 teaspoon sugar

1 teaspoon no-salt-added prepared mustard

1½ pounds fresh kale or Swiss chard, trimmed and chopped

SERVES 6	
Per Serving:	
Calories	329
Fat	14g
Sodium	113mg
Carbohydrates	14g
Fiber	2g
Sugar	2g
Protein	33g

1. Preheat oven to 400°F. Line a rimmed baking sheet with foil and set aside.
2. Trim and cut steak into 6 portions. Season both sides with rosemary and ½ teaspoon pepper.
3. Heat oil in a heavy skillet over medium-high heat. Place steaks in the skillet and cook until nicely browned, 3–4 minutes per side. Remove from heat and transfer steaks to the prepared baking sheet. Place on middle rack in oven and roast 5 minutes. Remove from oven and set aside.
4. Meanwhile, return the skillet to medium-high heat. Add wine and cook, scraping up any browned bits from the bottom of the pan, for 3 minutes. Add garlic, vinegar, sugar, mustard, and remaining ¼ teaspoon pepper and stir to combine.
5. Add kale and toss to coat. Cover the skillet and cook, stirring once or twice, until tender, about 5 minutes.
6. Transfer steaks to plates and top with kale. Serve immediately.

Barbecue Pizza with Ground Pork, Peppers, and Pineapple

SERVES 4

Per Serving:

Calories	306
Fat	7g
Sodium	98mg
Carbohydrates	39g
Fiber	5g
Sugar	12g
Protein	21g

This pizza has so much flavor, you won't believe it's salt-free!

1 cup white whole-wheat flour

1 teaspoon salt-free all-purpose seasoning

1 teaspoon salt-free Italian seasoning

½ teaspoon garlic powder

2 large egg whites

⅔ cup low-fat milk

½ pound lean ground pork

2 teaspoons salt-free chili seasoning

1 medium red onion, peeled and chopped

½ cup Spicy, Sweet, and Tangy Barbecue Sauce (see recipe in Chapter 4)

1 cup diced fresh pineapple

1 small red bell pepper, seeded and diced

1 small jalapeño pepper, seeded and minced

3 cloves garlic, peeled and minced

2 tablespoons chopped fresh cilantro

¼ cup shredded Swiss cheese

1 Preheat oven to 425°F. Grease and flour a 12" nonstick pizza pan and set aside.

2 Place flour, all-purpose seasoning, Italian seasoning, and garlic powder in a medium bowl and whisk to combine.

3 Stir in egg whites and milk. Pour batter into the prepared pizza pan and set aside.

4 Place a large skillet over medium heat. Add ground pork, chili seasoning, and onion and cook, stirring, for 5 minutes. Remove from heat and carefully drain any excess fat.

5 Spoon mixture evenly over the batter in the pan. Place pan on middle rack in oven and bake for 20 minutes.

6 Spread barbecue sauce evenly over pizza, then top with pineapple, peppers, garlic, and chopped cilantro. Sprinkle Swiss cheese over pizza.

7 Return pan to oven and bake for 3–5 minutes until cheese has melted.

8 Remove pizza from oven. Gently remove from pan and cut into 8 slices. Serve immediately.

Beef and Bean Burritos

SERVES 4

Per Serving:

Calories	605
Fat	10g
Sodium	285mg
Carbohydrates	94g
Fiber	8g
Sugar	11g
Protein	42g

CUT THE FAT

When choosing ground beef or other meats, always buy the leanest cuts possible. When you compare fat for a 4-ounce serving of ground beef, for instance, you can cut your fat intake in half simply by opting for the slightly more expensive 95 percent lean (5.6g fat) over the 90 percent lean (11g fat). Leaner meat may be more expensive, but better health is worth the small investment.

These hearty meal-sized burritos are so tasty, you'll hardly believe they're low-sodium. Store any leftover filling in the refrigerator and it'll be as good or even better the next day.

1 pound extra-lean ground beef

1 medium onion, peeled and minced

1 small jalapeño pepper, seeded and minced

2 cloves garlic, peeled and minced

1 (15-ounce) can no-salt-added black beans, drained and rinsed

⅔ cup fresh or frozen corn kernels

1 tablespoon no-salt-added tomato ketchup

1 tablespoon no-salt-added tomato paste

1 teaspoon honey

¾ teaspoon liquid smoke

1½ teaspoons ground cumin

1 teaspoon ground paprika

½ teaspoon ground coriander

½ teaspoon ground mustard

4 Garden City All Natural Lavash Whole Wheat Roll-Ups

1 cup low-sodium tomato salsa

½ cup nonfat sour cream

¼ cup chopped fresh cilantro

1 Brown ground beef in a medium skillet over medium heat. Add onion, jalapeño, and garlic and sauté for 5 minutes.

2 Add beans, corn, ketchup, tomato paste, honey, liquid smoke, cumin, paprika, coriander, and mustard. Reduce heat to medium-low and cook for 10 minutes, stirring frequently. Remove from heat.

3 Place lavash on a flat surface and divide filling evenly among them. Top each with 4 tablespoons salsa, 2 tablespoons sour cream, and 1 tablespoon chopped cilantro.

4 Fold the top and bottom of the roll-up toward the filling, fold one of the sides over the filling to cover, and then carefully roll to close. Repeat with remaining burritos. Serve immediately.

Asian-Inspired Mini Meatloaves with Salt-Free Hoisin Glaze

Deliciously meaty, these seductive little loaves are loaded with vegetables and the flavors of ginger, garlic, and 5-spice powder.

½ pound lean ground pork

1 medium red bell pepper, seeded and diced

¾ cup shelled edamame

3 scallions, sliced

3 cloves garlic, peeled and minced

1 tablespoon minced fresh ginger

1 large egg white

⅓ cup salt-free bread crumbs

½ teaspoon ground 5-spice powder

¼ teaspoon ground white pepper

3 tablespoons Faux Soy Sauce (see recipe in Chapter 4), divided

1 tablespoon no-salt-added tomato paste

1 Preheat oven to 375°F. Spray four cups of a jumbo muffin tin lightly with nonstick cooking spray and set aside.

2 Place pork, bell pepper, edamame, scallions, garlic, ginger, egg white, bread crumbs, 5-spice powder, and white pepper in a large bowl. Add 1 tablespoon Faux Soy Sauce and mix together using a wooden spoon or your hands.

3 Divide mixture into 4 equal portions and press into the prepared muffin tin.

4 Measure remaining 2 tablespoons Faux Soy Sauce and tomato paste in a small bowl and stir until smooth. Brush onto the tops of the meatloaves, dividing evenly.

5 Place muffin tin on middle rack in oven and bake for 30 minutes.

6 Remove from oven, gently run a knife around the sides of each loaf, and remove from tin. Serve immediately.

SERVES 4	
Per Serving:	
Calories	205
Fat	6g
Sodium	56mg
Carbohydrates	20g
Fiber	3g
Sugar	7g
Protein	17g

Whole-Grain Rotini with Pork, Pumpkin, and Sage

SERVES 6

Per Serving:

Calories	331
Fat	7g
Sodium	48mg
Carbohydrates	45g
Fiber	8g
Sugar	3g
Protein	23g

Pumpkin adds color, nutrients, and subtle flavor to this deliciously filling dish. Rotini, corkscrew-shaped pasta with a lot of surface area, allows the sauce to really cling. Feel free to substitute a different variety of pasta if you prefer.

1 (13-ounce) package whole-grain rotini

1 pound lean ground pork

1 medium red onion, peeled and diced

3 cloves garlic, peeled and minced

1 medium bell pepper, seeded and diced

1 cup pumpkin purée

2 teaspoons ground sage

1 teaspoon ground rosemary

½ teaspoon ground black pepper

1 Cook pasta according to package directions, omitting salt. Drain and set aside.

2 Heat a medium skillet over medium heat. Add ground pork, onion, and garlic and sauté for 2 minutes. Add bell pepper and sauté for 5 minutes.

3 Remove from heat. Add pasta, pumpkin, sage, rosemary, and black pepper to the skillet. Stir to combine. Serve immediately.

Ginger and Garlic Pork Stir-Fry

Intensely flavorful and speedy to prepare, this low-sodium stir-fry features tender pork loin and crisp vegetables in a delectable sauce. Serve it over cooked brown rice.

8 ounces pork tenderloin, thinly sliced

1½ tablespoons minced fresh ginger

3 cloves garlic, peeled and minced

2 tablespoons Faux Soy Sauce (see recipe in Chapter 4)

¾ cup low-sodium vegetable broth

2 teaspoons cornstarch

2 teaspoons sesame oil

1 head bok choy, sliced

½ pound pea pods or sugar snap peas, trimmed

2 medium carrots, peeled and sliced

1 medium red bell pepper, seeded and diced

1 small red onion, peeled and diced

4 scallions, sliced

¼ teaspoon ground black pepper

SERVES 4	
Per Serving:	
Calories	180
Fat	4g
Sodium	323mg
Carbohydrates	20g
Fiber	5g
Sugar	10g
Protein	17g

1 Place pork in a large bowl. Add ginger, garlic, and Faux Soy Sauce and stir to coat. Set aside.

2 In a small bowl, whisk together broth and cornstarch. Set aside.

3 Heat oil in a wok over medium heat. Add bok choy, pea pods, carrots, bell pepper, and onion and cook, stirring, for 5 minutes.

4 Add pork mixture and cook, stirring, for 5 minutes. Add broth mixture and cook, stirring, until sauce thickens, 30 seconds to 1 minute.

5 Remove from heat. Stir in scallions and season with black pepper. Serve immediately.

Pork Chops with Sautéed Apples and Shallots

Fill your house with the heavenly smell of apples and cinnamon. These boneless medallions in a white wine sauce are low in sodium and delicious.

1 pound pork loin chops

1 teaspoon ground black pepper, divided

1 teaspoon olive oil

3 small shallots, peeled and minced, divided

¾ cup white wine

2 tablespoons unsalted butter

4 medium apples, cored and thinly sliced

½ cup apple juice

¼ cup light brown sugar

½ teaspoon ground cinnamon

1. Preheat oven to 350°F.
2. Season chops with ½ teaspoon pepper. Heat oil in a large skillet over medium-high heat. Place chops in skillet and brown quickly on both sides, 2–3 minutes. Remove from skillet and transfer to a medium baking dish.
3. Reduce heat to medium. Add two of the minced shallots to skillet and cook, stirring, for 2–3 minutes, scraping pan to remove drippings.
4. Add wine and remaining ½ teaspoon pepper. Cook, stirring, for 1 minute, then pour over chops.
5. Cover baking dish with foil, place on middle rack in oven, and bake for 30 minutes, until internal temperature reaches 145°F.
6. Meanwhile, melt butter in a medium skillet over medium heat. Add the remaining minced shallot and sauté for 2 minutes. Add apples, apple juice, brown sugar, and cinnamon. Cook, stirring, for 10–15 minutes until apples are tender.
7. Remove skillet from heat. Remove pork chops from oven. Plate each chop with ¼ of the sautéed apple mixture. Serve immediately.

SERVES 4

Per Serving:

Calories	396
Fat	11g
Sodium	277mg
Carbohydrates	40g
Fiber	2g
Sugar	32g
Protein	28g

PORK FACTS

Lean pork is considered a healthy meat, containing roughly the same cholesterol per serving as chicken and turkey. It is an excellent source of protein, vitamins B_6 and B_{12}, and minerals. Its mild flavor is a great partner to most types of fruit, both fresh and dried. As a lean meat, pork can dry out quickly, so it's important not to overcook.

CHAPTER 8

Fish and Seafood

Roasted Salmon with Lemon, Mustard, and Dill

SERVES 4

Per Serving:

Calories	163
Fat	7g
Sodium	50mg
Carbohydrates	<1g
Fiber	0g
Sugar	0g
Protein	22g

Salmon is best without a lot of fanfare. Here it's roasted simply with a delectably tart and tangy dill glaze.

1 pound salmon fillet

3 tablespoons lemon juice

2 tablespoons no-salt-added prepared mustard

2 tablespoons chopped fresh dill

¼ teaspoon ground black pepper

1 Preheat oven to 450°F.
2 Slice salmon into 4 equal pieces and arrange in a baking pan.
3 Combine the remaining ingredients in a small bowl and brush tops and sides of fillets with mixture. Drizzle any remaining marinade over the top of the fillets.
4 Place pan on middle rack in oven and bake for 10–15 minutes, depending upon thickness of fillets. Salmon is done when it flakes easily with a fork.
5 Remove from oven and serve immediately.

Baked Tuna Cakes

This moist and healthy twist on crab cakes is accented with vegetables and a crisp oven-fried crust.

2 (5-ounce) cans no-salt-added tuna in water, drained

1 small carrot, peeled and shredded

1 stalk celery, finely diced

1 small shallot, peeled and minced

2 cloves garlic, peeled and minced

1 large egg white

¼ cup salt-free bread crumbs

2 tablespoons Salt-Free Mayonnaise (see recipe in Chapter 4)

½ teaspoon dried dill

½ teaspoon dried thyme

¼ teaspoon ground rosemary

¼ teaspoon ground black pepper

1 Preheat oven to 400°F. Spray a baking sheet lightly with nonstick cooking spray and set aside.

2 Place all ingredients in a medium bowl and stir to combine. Shape mixture into 4 patties and place on the prepared baking sheet.

3 Place baking sheet on middle rack in oven and bake 10 minutes. Remove from oven, gently flip, and bake 5 minutes more. Remove from oven and serve immediately.

SERVES 4

Per Serving:

Calories	163
Fat	5g
Sodium	66mg
Carbohydrates	8g
Fiber	1g
Sugar	1g
Protein	20g

COOKING SPRAY

Cut fat from your diet simply by using a cooking spray. Cooking spray is oil in an aerated form; when sprayed it provides a nonstick surface, and the amount of oil is so small as to be negligible. You can buy cooking spray in a can, but you can also make your own. Refillable oil spray bottles are sold at many kitchen stores and online. These can be used indefinitely, are chemical-free, and can be filled with your choice of oil.

Ahi Tuna with Grape Tomato Salsa

Fish always makes a fresh, light, and easy main course, and it's naturally very low in sodium! This recipe calls for broiling the tuna, but it also tastes great grilled. When grilling, 2 minutes per side should be more than enough. Tuna will become tough quickly if overcooked, so be careful.

SERVES 4

Per Serving:

Calories	174
Fat	4g
Sodium	48mg
Carbohydrates	4g
Fiber	1g
Sugar	2g
Protein	27g

YELLOWFIN TUNA

Yellowfin tuna, also known as ahi, live in the warm waters of the equator and can grow as large as 300 to 400 pounds. Yellowfin tuna is an excellent source of protein, vitamins B_6 and B_{12}, minerals, and omega-3 fatty acids. It's low in sodium, fat, and calories, making it a great choice on the DASH diet.

2 cups halved grape tomatoes

¼ cup finely diced onion

¼ cup finely diced green bell pepper

1 clove garlic, peeled and minced

1 tablespoon apple cider vinegar

1 tablespoon chopped fresh cilantro

½ teaspoon ground cumin

¼ teaspoon ground coriander

½ teaspoon ground black pepper, divided

⅛ teaspoon dried red pepper flakes

1 pound ahi (yellowfin) tuna, cut into 4 steaks

1 tablespoon olive oil, divided

1 Place tomatoes, onion, bell pepper, garlic, vinegar, cilantro, cumin, coriander, ¼ teaspoon black pepper, and red pepper flakes in a medium bowl and stir to combine. Set aside.

2 Preheat broiler. Place tuna steaks on a broiler pan or in a shallow baking dish, brush with ½ tablespoon olive oil, and sprinkle with ⅛ teaspoon black pepper. Place on top rack in oven and broil for 4 minutes.

3 Remove pan from oven and carefully flip steaks. Brush with remaining ½ tablespoon oil, sprinkle with remaining ⅛ teaspoon black pepper, and return to oven. Broil for another 4 minutes.

4 Remove from oven. Serve immediately with tomato salsa.

Tuna Noodle Casserole

SERVES 6

Per Serving:

Calories	434
Fat	9g
Sodium	137mg
Carbohydrates	55g
Fiber	4g
Sugar	4g
Protein	29g

Classic American comfort food at its best, tuna casserole is a great make-ahead meal: Assemble it in the morning or the night before, cover and refrigerate it, then pop it in the oven when you're ready to eat. If you can't find Bragg Organic Sea Kelp Delight Seasoning, substitute your favorite salt-free all-purpose seasoning.

1 pound whole-grain yolkless egg noodles

2 teaspoons canola oil

10 ounces button mushrooms, sliced

2 medium carrots, peeled and diced

2 stalks celery, diced

1 medium bell pepper, seeded and diced

1 medium onion, peeled and diced

4 cloves garlic, peeled and minced

2 (6-ounce) cans no-salt-added tuna in water, drained

1 cup nonfat sour cream

½ cup shredded Swiss cheese

1 teaspoon Bragg Organic Sea Kelp Delight Seasoning

½ teaspoon dried herbes de Provence

¼ teaspoon ground black pepper

1 Cook noodles according to package directions, omitting salt. Drain and set aside.

2 Preheat oven to 375°F. Spray a 3-quart baking dish lightly with nonstick cooking spray and set aside.

3 Heat oil in a medium skillet over medium heat. Add mushrooms, carrots, celery, bell pepper, onion, and garlic and cook, stirring, for 5 minutes. Remove from heat.

4 Add noodles, tuna, sour cream, cheese, seasoning, herbes de Provence, and black pepper and stir to combine.

5 Pour mixture into the prepared dish and cover with a lid or foil. Place on middle rack in oven and bake for 25 minutes.

6 Remove from oven and serve immediately.

Healthy Fish and Chips

This healthy version of the beloved coastal dinner is baked rather than fried. Choose your favorite white-fleshed fish, such as haddock, pollock, or cod. Serve this with lemon wedges, malt vinegar, and salt-free ketchup. Adapted from Let's Cook!

2 tablespoons unbleached all-purpose flour

2 tablespoons white whole-wheat flour

1 teaspoon ground black pepper, divided

2 large egg whites

2 cups salt-free bread crumbs or panko

1 teaspoon dried parsley

1 teaspoon dried dill

1 teaspoon dried thyme

1 pound white-fleshed fish, cut into 8 pieces

4 large potatoes, cut into 8 wedges each

3 tablespoons olive oil

1. Preheat oven to 425°F. Cover a large baking sheet with foil and set aside.
2. Measure flours into a wide, shallow bowl, add ½ teaspoon pepper, and whisk to combine.
3. Place egg whites in a second shallow bowl.
4. Place bread crumbs (or panko), parsley, dill, and thyme in a large zip-top plastic bag. Seal the bag and shake well.
5. Dredge each fillet completely in seasoned flour, then dip in egg, coating completely.
6. Place one fillet in the plastic bag, seal, and shake gently to coat. Carefully remove fillet from the bag and place on the prepared baking sheet. Repeat the process until all pieces are coated. Place the tray of fish in the refrigerator.
7. Line a large baking sheet with parchment paper. Arrange potato wedges on the baking sheet and brush both sides with oil. Sprinkle with remaining ½ teaspoon pepper.
8. Place the baking sheet on the middle rack in the oven and bake for 15 minutes. Remove from oven and flip potatoes over. Return to oven.
9. Remove fish from the refrigerator and place it on the top rack in the oven. Bake potatoes and fish for 15 minutes until both are crispy and brown. Remove from oven and serve immediately.

SERVES 4

Per Serving:

Calories	534
Fat	13g
Sodium	142mg
Carbohydrates	65g
Fiber	5g
Sugar	5g
Protein	38g

LOW-SODIUM TARTAR SAUCE

Whip up a batch of low-sodium tartar sauce in minutes by combining ¼ cup Salt-Free Mayonnaise (see recipe in Chapter 4) with a tablespoon of salt-free pickle relish. Use immediately or cover and refrigerate until serving. Salt-free pickle relish is sold at select stores and online.

Roasted Steelhead Trout with Grapefruit Sauce

SERVES 4

Per Serving:

Calories	250
Fat	7g
Sodium	36mg
Carbohydrates	22g
Fiber	2g
Sugar	16g
Protein	24g

The fish is roasted simply; just a brush of olive oil and dusting of black pepper is all it takes to make it melt in your mouth. But the sauce elevates it to stardom. The combination of citrus tang, sweetness, and spice is stupendous. Adapted from Fine Cooking.

1 pound steelhead trout

3 teaspoons olive oil, divided

¼ teaspoon ground black pepper

2 medium ruby red grapefruits

1 medium shallot, peeled and minced

1 clove garlic, peeled and minced

1 teaspoon minced fresh ginger

2 teaspoons agave nectar

⅛ teaspoon ground cayenne pepper

2 tablespoons thinly sliced fresh basil

1. Preheat oven to 350°F.
2. Place trout in a baking dish, brush with 2 teaspoons oil, and sprinkle with pepper. Place the dish on the middle rack in the oven and roast for 15 minutes.
3. Meanwhile, cut the top and bottom off one grapefruit. Stand on one end and cut down to remove the white pith and peel. Use a sharp knife to remove each grapefruit segment from its membrane. Cut the segments in half and set aside. Juice the remaining grapefruit and set aside.
4. Heat the remaining 1 teaspoon oil in a small saucepan over medium heat. Add shallot and garlic and sauté for 2 minutes.
5. Add ginger, grapefruit juice, agave nectar, and cayenne and stir to combine. Bring to a simmer, then cook until reduced by half, about 10 minutes.
6. Remove saucepan from heat. Stir in grapefruit and basil.
7. Remove trout from oven. Slice into 4 portions, top with sauce, and serve immediately.

Spicy Tilapia with Pineapple Relish

Tilapia is mild in flavor, meaty, and often inexpensive. This recipe calls for salt-free Cajun seasoning—try Benson's Salt-Free Calypso or Mrs. Dash Caribbean Citrus. For those with an aversion to spicy food, omit the red pepper flakes and jalapeño. Adapted from Cooking Light.

½ medium pineapple, peeled, cored, and diced

1 small red onion, peeled and diced

1 small tomato, diced

1 small jalapeño pepper, seeded and minced

2 cloves garlic, peeled and minced

2 tablespoons plain unflavored rice vinegar

2 tablespoons chopped fresh cilantro

2 teaspoons canola oil

1 teaspoon salt-free Cajun seasoning

¼ teaspoon dried red pepper flakes

1 pound boneless tilapia fillets

1 Combine pineapple, onion, tomato, jalapeño, and garlic in a medium bowl. Add vinegar and cilantro and stir to combine.

2 Heat oil in a large skillet over medium-high heat.

3 Combine Cajun seasoning and red pepper flakes in a small bowl and sprinkle evenly over fish fillets. Place fish in skillet and cook for 2 minutes per side, or until fish flakes easily when tested with a fork.

4 Remove from heat and serve immediately with pineapple relish.

SERVES 4	
Per Serving:	
Calories	220
Fat	4g
Sodium	68mg
Carbohydrates	22g
Fiber	2g
Sugar	16g
Protein	24g

Southwestern Salmon

The colorful seasoning mix is as pretty as it is flavorful, and the resulting fish is crisp, juicy, and delicious.

1 teaspoon dried cilantro

1 teaspoon ground cumin

1 teaspoon ground paprika

½ teaspoon ground black pepper

½ teaspoon ground coriander

⅛ teaspoon ground cayenne pepper

1 pound salmon fillet

1 Preheat broiler and move a rack to the top of the oven. Spray a baking sheet lightly with nonstick cooking spray and set aside.

2 Place cilantro, cumin, paprika, black pepper, coriander, and cayenne pepper in a small bowl and stir to combine.

3 Sprinkle spice mixture over salmon fillet and gently rub mixture into fish. Place fillet on the prepared baking sheet.

4 Place the baking sheet on the top rack in the oven and broil for about 7 minutes, 1–2 minutes less for thin fillets, a little longer for thicker fillets. When cooked fully, salmon will be opaque and flake easily.

5 Remove baking sheet from oven, slice salmon into 4 portions, and serve immediately.

SERVES 4

Per Serving:

Calories	171
Fat	8g
Sodium	50mg
Carbohydrates	0g
Fiber	0g
Sugar	0g
Protein	22g

SAVORY BROILED SALMON

For a different take on this spicy salmon, combine 1 teaspoon dried marjoram, ½ teaspoon each dried savory and ground white pepper, and ¼ teaspoon each dried thyme, ground rosemary, and garlic powder in a small bowl. Rub the mixture into a 1-pound boneless salmon fillet, then broil 7–8 minutes. The rub adds an extra jolt of flavor to an already tasty fish, and the broiling process renders the flesh crisp outside and juicy within.

Salmon Cakes

Delicately crisp outside and flavorfully moist inside, these Salmon Cakes are a real treat whether sandwiched in rolls or eaten plain.

MAYONNAISE SUBSTITUTE

Instead of adding salt-free mayonnaise to a recipe, try substituting an equal amount of plain nonfat Greek yogurt. Its thick and creamy consistency works well in many types of salads and sandwiches, from tuna and salmon to chicken and egg. To thin the yogurt, add a little lemon juice or low-sodium broth. For added flavor, add minced garlic and some chopped fresh herbs.

1 (15-ounce) can no-salt-added boneless salmon, drained

4 tablespoons Salt-Free Mayonnaise (see recipe in Chapter 4)

½ cup salt-free bread crumbs

1 small onion, peeled and minced

1 small bell pepper, seeded and minced

1 large egg white

1 teaspoon dried herbes de Provence

½ teaspoon ground paprika

¼ teaspoon ground mustard

⅛ teaspoon celery seed

¼ teaspoon ground black pepper

1 Preheat oven to 400°F. Spray a baking sheet lightly with nonstick cooking spray and set aside.

2 Place all ingredients in a large bowl. Mix using a spoon or your hands. Divide mixture into 6 equal portions and shape into patties.

3 Place patties on the prepared baking sheet. Place baking sheet on middle rack in oven and bake for 10 minutes. Remove from oven, gently flip, and return to oven to bake 5 minutes more.

4 Remove from oven and serve immediately.

Open-Faced Tuna Melts

This lightened version of the beloved diner sandwich uses home-made salt-free mayonnaise, leaving the sandwiches lower in sodium, fat, and cholesterol.

1 (5-ounce) can no-salt-added tuna in water, drained

1 small shallot, peeled and finely chopped

1 stalk celery, finely diced

1 small carrot, peeled and finely diced

2 tablespoons Salt-Free Mayonnaise (see recipe in Chapter 4)

¼ cup chopped Sweet and Spicy Salt-Free Pickles (see recipe in Chapter 3)

½ teaspoon dried herbes de Provence

¼ teaspoon ground black pepper

2 slices low-sodium bread

2 slices romaine lettuce

1 small tomato, sliced

2 slices Swiss cheese

1 Preheat broiler.

2 Place tuna in a medium bowl. Add shallot, celery, carrot, mayonnaise, pickles, herbes de Provence, and pepper and stir to combine.

3 Place bread slices on a baking sheet. Top each with a lettuce slice and half the tuna mixture. Smooth to even and top with sliced tomato and cheese.

4 Broil sandwiches for 1–2 minutes until cheese melts. Serve immediately.

SERVES 2	
Per Serving:	
Calories	368
Fat	18g
Sodium	130mg
Carbohydrates	21g
Fiber	1g
Sugar	4g
Protein	29g

HERBES DE PROVENCE

A classic blend of French herbs, typically composed of dried basil, thyme, savory, fennel, and lavender, herbes de Provence gives a distinct flavor to many dishes and is particularly well suited to grilled meats and seafood. Commercial blends are sold in supermarkets and online.

Shrimp Creole

SERVES 6

Per Serving:

Calories	152
Fat	3g
Sodium	136mg
Carbohydrates	11g
Fiber	2g
Sugar	6g
Protein	17g

THE SKINNY ON SHRIMP

Shrimp are fairly high in sodium naturally, at roughly 160 milligrams per 3-ounce serving, so they should be consumed carefully. Shrimp come in a variety of sizes, from miniscule to extra colossal, and are typically sold by weight and size; for instance, a pound of large shrimp contains roughly 30 to 35 pieces. Most shrimp consumed in the United States have been processed to some degree and may have added salt. Read package labels carefully and buy fresh, unprocessed shrimp whenever possible.

This spicy and beautiful shrimp dish is made for special occasions. Serve it over brown or white rice.

2 teaspoons canola oil

1 medium onion, peeled and thinly sliced

1 medium bell pepper, seeded and thinly sliced

2 stalks celery, thinly sliced

3 cloves garlic, peeled and minced

2 (15-ounce) cans no-salt-added diced tomatoes

1 (8-ounce) can no-salt-added tomato sauce

⅓ cup white wine

½ teaspoon apple cider vinegar

2 bay leaves

2 teaspoons salt-free chili seasoning

1 teaspoon ground paprika

½ teaspoon ground black pepper

⅛ teaspoon ground cayenne pepper

1 pound large shrimp, peeled

1 Heat oil in a medium skillet over medium heat. Add onion, bell pepper, celery, and garlic and cook, stirring, for 5 minutes.

2 Add tomatoes, tomato sauce, wine, vinegar, bay leaves, chili seasoning, paprika, black pepper, and cayenne pepper and stir to combine. Simmer for 10 minutes, stirring frequently. Cover and reduce heat to medium-low if sauce begins to splatter.

3 Stir in shrimp and simmer for 5 minutes.

4 Remove from heat and remove bay leaves from pan. Serve immediately.

CHAPTER 9

Chicken and Turkey

Grilled Tequila Chicken with Sautéed Peppers and Onion

SERVES 4

Per Serving:

Calories	259
Fat	3g
Sodium	118mg
Carbohydrates	18g
Fiber	1g
Sugar	7g
Protein	28g

This fabulous chicken is succulently moist and unbelievably flavorful thanks to the tequila marinade. The longer the chicken steeps, the greater the flavor. Serve the chicken with fresh corn on the cob, nonfat sour cream, and chopped fresh cilantro.

1 cup lime juice

⅓ cup tequila

3 cloves garlic, peeled and chopped

¼ cup chopped fresh cilantro

1 tablespoon agave nectar

½ teaspoon ground black pepper

1 teaspoon ground cumin

½ teaspoon ground coriander

4 (4-ounce) boneless, skinless chicken breasts

2 teaspoons canola oil

1 large green bell pepper, seeded and diced

1 large red bell pepper, seeded and diced

1 large onion, peeled and diced

½ cup nonfat sour cream

1 Place lime juice, tequila, garlic, cilantro, agave nectar, black pepper, cumin, and coriander in a large bowl and whisk to combine.

2 Add chicken and turn several times to coat. Cover and refrigerate. Marinate for at least 6 hours, preferably overnight.

3 Heat a gas or charcoal grill. Grill chicken until no longer pink but still juicy and tender, 10–15 minutes per side.

4 Meanwhile, heat oil in a medium skillet over medium heat. Add peppers and onion and sauté for 5 minutes. Remove from heat.

5 Remove chicken from grill. Serve immediately with sautéed vegetables and a dollop of sour cream.

Chicken, Black Bean, and Veggie Soft Tacos

Soft corn tortillas are filled with a saucy and spicy combination of chicken, vegetables, and beans. If you're using a commercial chili seasoning, start with a teaspoon and work up from there.

½ cup low-sodium chicken broth

1 medium carrot, diced

1 medium sweet potato, peeled and diced

3 boneless, skinless chicken thighs, cut into bite-sized pieces

1 medium onion, peeled and diced

1 medium bell pepper, diced

1 jalapeño pepper, seeded and minced

3 cloves garlic, peeled and minced

1 (15-ounce) can no-salt-added black beans, undrained

½ cup corn kernels

2 tablespoons no-salt-added tomato paste

2 tablespoons Salt-Free Chili Seasoning (see recipe in Chapter 4)

12 (5") corn tortillas, warmed

½ cup nonfat sour cream

¼ cup chopped fresh cilantro

1 Heat a medium skillet over medium heat. Add broth, carrot, and sweet potato, cover the pan, and cook for 5 minutes. Add chicken, onion, peppers, and garlic. Cover and cook for another 5 minutes, stirring once halfway through cooking time.

2 Add beans with liquid, corn, tomato paste, and chili seasoning to the skillet. Cook, stirring, for 5 minutes.

3 Remove from heat. Spoon filling into tortillas and top with sour cream and cilantro.

4 Serve immediately.

SERVES 6

Per Serving:

Calories	338
Fat	3g
Sodium	90mg
Carbohydrates	63g
Fiber	9g
Sugar	5g
Protein	17g

SALT-FREE CHILI SEASONING

Not all salt-free seasoning blends are the same, and nowhere is this more apparent than when it comes to chili seasonings. Some brands are fiery, while others are fairly bland. Taste seasonings before adding them to food. Carefully assess how much or how little needs to be added to your food and you'll never risk overseasoning.

Saucy Barbecued Chicken with Rice

This simple and satisfying low-sodium chicken recipe is full of barbecue flavor and amazingly tender meat. Try it spooned over baked potatoes instead of rice.

1 teaspoon canola oil

1 small onion, peeled and finely diced

2 cloves garlic, peeled and minced

1 pound boneless, skinless chicken thighs, cut into bite-sized pieces

1 large bell pepper, seeded and diced

2 (8-ounce) cans no-salt-added tomato sauce

2 tablespoons apple cider vinegar

2 tablespoons molasses

1 tablespoon honey

1 teaspoon liquid smoke

1½ teaspoons ground cumin

1 teaspoon ground paprika

½ teaspoon dried oregano

½ teaspoon ground black pepper

¼ teaspoon ground cayenne pepper

¼ cup chopped fresh cilantro

4 cups cooked brown rice

SERVES 4	
Per Serving:	
Calories	474
Fat	7g
Sodium	126mg
Carbohydrates	70g
Fiber	6g
Sugar	18g
Protein	29g

1 Heat oil in a medium skillet over medium heat. Add onion and garlic and sauté for 2 minutes. Add chicken and bell pepper and sauté for 2 minutes more.

2 Stir in tomato sauce, vinegar, molasses, honey, liquid smoke, cumin, paprika, oregano, black pepper, and cayenne and stir to combine. Bring to a boil.

3 Reduce heat to medium-low, cover, and simmer until chicken is cooked through, 10–15 minutes.

4 Remove from heat. Stir in cilantro. Serve immediately over rice.

Oven-Baked Chicken Tenders

SERVES 8

Per Serving:

Calories	266
Fat	2g
Sodium	132mg
Carbohydrates	13g
Fiber	1g
Sugar	1g
Protein	45g

Baked rather than fried, these crispy tenders are much lower in fat than the frozen kind, but have a whole lot of flavor. They freeze wonderfully; place leftovers in an airtight container for later meals. Serve them with salt-free ketchup, barbecue sauce, and honey for dipping.

½ cup unbleached all-purpose flour

½ cup white whole-wheat flour

½ cup salt-free bread crumbs

2 teaspoons garlic powder

2 teaspoons onion powder

1 teaspoon ground paprika

1 teaspoon ground black pepper

½ cup low-fat milk

1 large egg white

3 pounds boneless, skinless chicken breast tenderloins

1 Preheat oven to 375°F. Line a large baking sheet with foil, spray lightly with nonstick cooking spray, and set aside.

2 Combine all-purpose flour, whole-wheat flour, bread crumbs, garlic powder, onion powder, paprika, and pepper in a large zip-top plastic bag. Seal and shake to combine.

3 Whisk together milk and egg white in a shallow bowl.

4 One piece at a time, dip chicken into the milk mixture, then place in the plastic bag with flour mixture, seal, and shake vigorously to coat. Place breaded tenders on the prepared baking sheet.

5 Place baking sheet on middle rack in oven and bake for 10–15 minutes, until golden brown.

6 Remove from oven and serve immediately.

Chicken with Rice, Lemon, and Kale

In this easy, oven-baked meal hearty kale, meaty chunks of chicken, and rice are bathed in a delicious lemony broth.

8 boneless, skinless chicken thighs, cut into bite-sized pieces

1 cup basmati rice

4 cups chopped fresh kale

2 medium shallots, peeled and chopped

2 cups low-sodium chicken broth

½ cup white wine

3 tablespoons lemon juice

1 tablespoon grated lemon zest

4 cloves garlic, peeled and minced

1 tablespoon fresh thyme or 1 teaspoon dried thyme

¼ teaspoon ground black pepper

1. Preheat oven to 425°F. Spray a 9" × 13" casserole pan lightly with nonstick cooking spray.
2. Arrange chicken in a single layer in the prepared pan. Scatter rice, kale, and shallots over the top.
3. Add broth, wine, lemon juice, zest, garlic, thyme, and pepper to a medium bowl and whisk to combine. Carefully pour the mixture over the contents of the pan.
4. Cover pan tightly with foil, then place on middle rack of oven and bake for 30 minutes. Remove from oven and serve immediately.

SERVES 4

Per Serving:

Calories	340
Fat	5g
Sodium	140mg
Carbohydrates	45g
Fiber	2g
Sugar	<1g
Protein	24g

COOKING WITH WINE

Wine can add depth and interest to many foods, and this is especially true when it comes to salt-free cooking. If you're wary of wine's intoxicating effects, add only to foods that will be heated. The cooking process evaporates the alcohol, leaving only its flavor behind. Fine wines are to be savored, and are best consumed by the glass. When cooking with wine, opt for inexpensive bottles.

Honey Mustard Chicken Breasts

SERVES 4	
Per Serving:	
Calories	170
Fat	1g
Sodium	103mg
Carbohydrates	9g
Fiber	0g
Sugar	8g
Protein	26g

This moist and flavorful recipe will leave you wanting more. These breasts can be cooked on a grill instead of in the oven. Grill them over medium heat, turning once, until chicken is slightly crisp outside and no longer pink inside, 10–15 minutes per side.

2 tablespoons mustard seeds

1 tablespoon ground mustard

1 tablespoon distilled white vinegar

2 tablespoons water

¼ cup white wine

2 tablespoons honey

1 pound boneless, skinless chicken breasts

1 Crush mustard seeds slightly using a mortar and pestle or small spice grinder. Place in a medium bowl or large zip-top bag. Add ground mustard, vinegar, water, wine, and honey and mix to combine.

2 Add chicken to the marinade and coat completely. Cover bowl or seal bag tightly and refrigerate for 4–12 hours.

3 Preheat oven to 375°F.

4 Remove chicken from marinade and place in a 9" × 13" baking dish. Drizzle with a little of the marinade. Cover dish tightly with foil.

5 Place pan on middle rack in oven and bake until chicken reaches an internal temperature of 160°F, about 30 minutes.

6 Remove from oven and serve immediately.

Chicken Curry with Creamy Tomato Sauce

This quick and easy chicken curry tastes terrific and will leave your house smelling glorious. Serve it over cooked basmati rice.

1 teaspoon canola oil

1 pound boneless, skinless chicken breasts, cut into bite-sized pieces

1 large onion, peeled and diced

3 cloves garlic, peeled and minced

1 tablespoon minced fresh ginger

1 small jalapeño pepper, seeded and minced

1 (15-ounce) can no-salt-added diced tomatoes

2 tablespoons no-salt-added tomato paste

¾ cup low-sodium chicken or vegetable broth

½ cup nonfat plain yogurt

2 teaspoons salt-free garam masala or curry powder

½ teaspoon ground paprika

¼ teaspoon ground black pepper

¼ cup chopped fresh cilantro

1 Heat oil in a large skillet over medium heat. Add chicken, onion, garlic, and ginger and cook, stirring, for 5 minutes. Add jalapeño, tomatoes with juice, tomato paste, broth, yogurt, garam masala (or curry powder), paprika, and black pepper and stir to combine. Bring to a boil.

2 Reduce heat to medium-low, cover, and simmer, stirring frequently, until chicken is fully cooked, about 20 minutes.

3 Remove from heat. Stir in cilantro and serve immediately.

SERVES 4	
Per Serving:	
Calories	189
Fat	3g
Sodium	130mg
Carbohydrates	10g
Fiber	1g
Sugar	6g
Protein	29g

CHICKEN FACTS

Chicken's mild flavor and affordable nature make it one of the most popular types of protein worldwide. When preparing chicken, first remove the skin; this will greatly reduce the amount of fat you're consuming. White meat contains less fat than dark meat, but dark meat contains a higher concentration of some nutrients. Skinless chicken is an excellent source of protein, vitamin B_6, and minerals.

Spicy Yogurt-Marinated Chicken Tenders

SERVES 4

Per Serving:

Calories	181
Fat	2g
Sodium	110mg
Carbohydrates	11g
Fiber	0g
Sugar	9g
Protein	28g

DIFFERENT TYPES OF MARINADES

Marinades can be divided into one of three types. Acidic marinades are those made with fruit juice, wine, or vinegar. Enzymatic marinades rely on fruit enzymes, such as those found in papaya, pineapple, or kiwi. Dairy-based marinades use either buttermilk or yogurt as their base. Of all three types, only dairy marinades reliably tenderize without the risk of toughening or disintegrating meat.

Although this recipe uses chicken tenders, the marinade works equally well with any cut of chicken, from bone-in breasts to a whole roaster. For maximum impact, allow the chicken to marinate as long as possible. Recipe adapted from www.stonyfield.com.

¾ cup nonfat plain yogurt

1 medium onion, peeled and minced

3 cloves garlic, peeled and minced

2 tablespoons lime juice

1 tablespoon honey

1 teaspoon ground paprika

1 teaspoon ground cumin

¼ teaspoon ground cayenne pepper

¼ teaspoon ground cinnamon

1 pound boneless, skinless chicken tenders

1 Place yogurt, onion, garlic, lime juice, honey, paprika, cumin, cayenne, and cinnamon in a large bowl and stir to combine. Add chicken and toss to coat. Cover and refrigerate 30 minutes to 12 hours.

2 Preheat oven to 375°F. Line a baking sheet with parchment paper or foil and arrange chicken in a single layer.

3 Place baking sheet on middle rack in oven and bake until golden brown, 10–15 minutes.

4 Remove from oven and serve immediately.

Low-Sodium Kung Pao Chicken

It's all here: the spicy bite of ginger, the tang of rice wine vinegar, and the smoky depth of sesame oil—that certain indescribable something that says "I am Chinese takeout"! Adapted from Fine Cooking.

1 cup low-sodium chicken broth

2 tablespoons Faux Soy Sauce (see recipe in Chapter 4)

1 tablespoon balsamic vinegar

5 tablespoons cornstarch, divided

2 teaspoons sesame oil

1 teaspoon sugar

1 pound boneless, skinless chicken breasts, cubed

¼ teaspoon ground black pepper

2 tablespoons canola oil, divided

¼ teaspoon dried red pepper flakes

2 tablespoons minced fresh ginger

6 scallions, sliced, whites and greens kept separate

1 medium red bell pepper, seeded and diced

2 stalks celery, sliced

2 medium carrots, peeled and sliced

¼ cup unseasoned rice vinegar

¼ cup chopped unsalted cashews or peanuts

SERVES 4	
Per Serving:	
Calories	347
Fat	14g
Sodium	135mg
Carbohydrates	24g
Fiber	2g
Sugar	8g
Protein	29g

1 Place broth, Faux Soy Sauce, balsamic vinegar, 1 tablespoon cornstarch, sesame oil, and sugar in a medium bowl. Whisk to combine and set aside.

2 Place chicken in a large bowl, add the remaining 4 tablespoons cornstarch and black pepper, and toss to coat.

3 Heat 1 tablespoon canola oil in a large skillet over medium heat. Add chicken mixture and cook until lightly browned on all sides, about 4 minutes total.

4 Add the remaining tablespoon canola oil to the skillet. Add red pepper flakes, ginger, and scallion whites and cook, stirring, for 1 minute. Add bell pepper, celery, and carrots and sauté until they soften slightly, about 2 minutes. Add vinegar and scrape the bottom of the skillet to incorporate any browned bits.

5 Give chicken broth mixture a quick whisk, then add to the skillet.

6 Cook, stirring, for 2 minutes more, then remove skillet from heat and serve immediately, sprinkled with nuts and scallion greens.

Tropical Chicken Salad Wrap Sandwiches

SERVES 6

Per Serving:

Calories	369
Fat	10g
Sodium	77mg
Carbohydrates	45g
Fiber	4g
Sugar	6g
Protein	30g

Colorfully festive with a fresh, spicy kick, these sandwiches make great party fare sliced in half and arranged on a platter. The filling eschews mayonnaise in favor of a light vinaigrette. Add sliced avocado to the wraps if you like.

1 pound boneless, skinless chicken breasts

1 medium mango, peeled, pitted, and diced

1 small red onion, peeled and diced

1 small bell pepper, seeded and diced

1 small jalapeño pepper, seeded and minced

2 cloves garlic, peeled and minced

1 cup canned no-salt-added black beans, drained and rinsed

2 tablespoons apple cider vinegar

2 tablespoons lime juice

2 tablespoons olive oil

¼ cup chopped fresh cilantro

½ teaspoon ground white pepper

4 cups mixed salad greens

6 Garden City All Natural Lavash Whole Wheat Roll-Ups

1 Place chicken breasts in a large saucepan and add enough water to cover. Bring to a boil over high heat. Reduce heat slightly and continue boiling about 20 minutes, until fully cooked.

2 Remove from heat, drain, and set aside to cool for 20 minutes.

3 Cut chicken into bite-sized pieces. Place in a large bowl and add the mango, onion, peppers, garlic, and beans.

4 Place vinegar, lime juice, oil, cilantro, and white pepper in a small bowl and whisk to combine. Pour over chicken mixture and stir to coat.

5 Divide greens and chicken salad evenly between lavash, then roll up sandwiches. Slice each sandwich in half using a sharp knife.

6 Serve immediately or cover and refrigerate until serving.

Grilled Chicken Patties

Per Serving:

Calories	118
Fat	2g
Sodium	73mg
Carbohydrates	1g
Fiber	0g
Sugar	0g
Protein	20g

KEEPING GRILLED BURGERS JUICY

Burgers have a tendency to round upward while cooking on the grill. To keep patties flat while cooking, make a small indentation in the center of each side using the back of a spoon or your thumb. The indented centers will rise to meet the rest of the burger, without the need for flattening. Grilled burgers will remain juicy and delicious.

Lean ground chicken plus southwestern spice make yummy burgers. And they're so low in sodium, you can splurge and sandwich them between regular whole-grain buns!

1 pound ground chicken

1 teaspoon ground paprika

½ teaspoon ground black pepper

½ teaspoon ground cumin

½ teaspoon salt-free chili seasoning

¼ teaspoon dried red pepper flakes

1 Preheat a gas or charcoal grill.
2 Place all ingredients in a medium bowl. Mix using a wooden spoon or your hands. Divide the mixture into 4 equal portions. Roll each portion into a ball, then flatten to form patties.
3 Place patties on the hot grill and cook for 5–6 minutes on the first side. Gently flip patties and grill for another 5–6 minutes on the second side.
4 Remove from grill and serve immediately.

Broccoli, Ground Turkey, and Pesto Pizza

Lean ground turkey, savory red onion, broccoli, and pesto make this a low-sodium pizza you won't forget. And it's ready in just 30 minutes!

1 cup white whole-wheat flour

1 teaspoon salt-free all-purpose seasoning

1 teaspoon salt-free Italian seasoning

½ teaspoon garlic powder

2 large egg whites

⅔ cup low-fat milk

½ pound lean ground turkey

1 medium red onion, peeled and chopped

1 teaspoon olive oil

1 medium red bell pepper, seeded and diced

1 medium head broccoli, chopped

4 tablespoons Basil Pesto (see recipe in Chapter 4)

½ cup shredded Swiss cheese

¼ teaspoon ground black pepper

SERVES 4	
Per Serving:	
Calories	327
Fat	14g
Sodium	131mg
Carbohydrates	30g
Fiber	5g
Sugar	4g
Protein	22g

1 Preheat oven to 425°F. Grease and flour a 12" nonstick pizza pan and set aside.

2 Place flour, all-purpose seasoning, Italian seasoning, and garlic powder in a medium bowl and whisk to combine. Stir in egg whites and milk. Pour batter into the prepared pizza pan and set aside.

3 Place a large skillet over medium heat. Add ground turkey and onion and cook, stirring, for 5 minutes.

4 Remove from heat and carefully drain any excess fat. Spoon mixture evenly over the batter in the pan. Place pan on middle rack of oven and bake for 20 minutes.

5 While pizza is baking, heat oil in a large skillet over medium heat. Add bell pepper and broccoli and sauté for 5 minutes. Remove skillet from heat and set aside.

6 Once crust is baked, remove pan from oven. Top pizza with pesto, spreading evenly. Arrange broccoli and peppers evenly over the top, then sprinkle with cheese and black pepper. Return pan to oven and bake for 3–5 minutes, until cheese has melted completely.

7 Remove pizza from oven. Gently remove from pan and cut into 8 slices. Serve immediately.

Ground Turkey Meatloaf Minis

SERVES 6

Per Serving:

Calories	251
Fat	7g
Sodium	112mg
Carbohydrates	21g
Fiber	2g
Sugar	7g
Protein	25g

HOMEMADE BREAD CRUMBS

To make your own salt-free bread crumbs, crisp several pieces of salt-free or low-sodium bread in the toaster or conventional oven. Tear or crumb the toasted bread into tiny pieces; for a fine crumb, pulse in a food processor. Wonderful low-sodium bread crumbs can also be made from finely chopped unsalted nuts, matzo, and salt-free potato chips.

A deliciously lighter version of the all-American meal, these mini meatloaves can also be made with lean ground chicken. Serve them with Garlic Rosemary Mashed Potatoes (see recipe in Chapter 11).

1½ pounds lean ground turkey

1 medium onion, peeled and finely diced

2 stalks celery, finely diced

1 small bell pepper, seeded and finely diced

4 cloves garlic, peeled and minced

1 (8-ounce) can no-salt-added tomato sauce

1 large egg white

¾ cup salt-free bread crumbs

1 tablespoon molasses

¼ teaspoon liquid smoke

½ teaspoon dried basil

½ teaspoon dried oregano

½ teaspoon dried savory

½ teaspoon dried thyme

½ teaspoon ground black pepper

¼ cup salt-free ketchup

1 Preheat oven to 375°F. Spray a six-cup jumbo muffin tin lightly with nonstick cooking spray and set aside.

2 Place ground turkey, onion, celery, bell pepper, garlic, tomato sauce, egg white, bread crumbs, molasses, liquid smoke, basil, oregano, savory, thyme, and black pepper in a large bowl and mix using a wooden spoon or your hands.

3 Divide mixture evenly between the muffin cups and press in firmly. Top meatloaves with ketchup and spread evenly.

4 Place muffin tin on middle rack in oven and bake for 30 minutes.

5 Remove from oven. Gently run a knife around the sides of each loaf and remove from tin. Serve immediately.

Turkey and Brown Rice–Stuffed Peppers

This healthier version of the comfort-food classic uses ground turkey and brown rice, with juicy tomatoes and raisins for a little added sweetness.

4 large bell peppers

1 pound lean ground turkey

1 medium onion, peeled and diced

3 cloves garlic, peeled and minced

2 stalks celery, diced

2 cups cooked brown rice

1 (15-ounce) can no-salt-added diced tomatoes

2 tablespoons no-salt-added tomato paste

¼ cup raisins

2 teaspoons ground cumin

1 teaspoon dried oregano

½ teaspoon ground cinnamon

½ teaspoon ground black pepper

SERVES 4	
Per Serving:	
Calories	354
Fat	8g
Sodium	126mg
Carbohydrates	45g
Fiber	6g
Sugar	14g
Protein	27g

1 Preheat oven to 425°F. Lightly spray a 9" × 13" baking dish with nonstick cooking spray and set aside.

2 Trim about ½" off the top of each pepper and set tops aside. Carefully core and seed, leaving the peppers intact. Trim bottoms if necessary so that peppers sit flat. Set aside.

3 Heat a medium skillet over medium heat. Add ground turkey, onion, garlic, and celery and sauté for 5 minutes. Remove from heat. Stir in the remaining ingredients.

4 Fill each pepper with ¼ of the mixture, pressing firmly to pack. Stand peppers in the prepared baking dish, replace the pepper tops, and then cover dish tightly with foil. Place dish on middle rack in oven and bake until tender, 25–30 minutes.

5 Remove from oven and serve immediately.

Seasoned Turkey Burgers with Sautéed Mushrooms and Swiss

These juicy, salt-free burgers will have you oohing and aahing your way to the last mushroom-topped bite.

1 pound lean ground turkey

2 cloves garlic, peeled and minced

1 tablespoon no-salt-added prepared mustard

2 teaspoons low-sodium Worcestershire sauce

1 teaspoon salt-free Italian seasoning

½ teaspoon ground black pepper

1 teaspoon olive oil

3 cups sliced mushrooms

4 Soft and Crusty No-Rise Rolls (see recipe in Chapter 11)

½ cup shredded Swiss cheese

1 Place ground turkey in a large bowl. Add garlic, mustard, Worcestershire sauce, Italian seasoning, and pepper and mix using your hands.

2 Divide mixture into 4 equal parts. Roll each portion into a round ball, then flatten and form into patties.

3 Grill or broil the burgers until they reach an internal temperature of 165°F. If grilling, they'll take 5–6 minutes per side; if broiling, they'll take 4–6 minutes per side. Remove burgers from heat, cover, and set aside.

4 Heat oil in a medium skillet over medium heat. Add mushrooms and sauté for 5 minutes. Remove from heat.

5 Sandwich each burger in a bun, dividing sautéed mushrooms and cheese evenly among them. Serve immediately.

SERVES 4

Per Serving:

Calories	377
Fat	14g
Sodium	145mg
Carbohydrates	31g
Fiber	3g
Sugar	3g
Protein	32g

AN EASY WAY TO CLEAN YOUR GRILL

Whether you own a charcoal or propane grill, the easiest way to clean it is right after use. After removing food from the grill, close the lid, and allow the flames to burn off excess grease and debris. After about 10 minutes, go back and scrape the grates with a heavy wire brush. Turn off the gas (if applicable) and close the lid again. The grill is now ready for your next cookout.

Lemon Thyme Turkey Meatballs

SERVES 6

Per Serving:

Calories	226
Fat	8g
Sodium	117mg
Carbohydrates	17g
Fiber	1g
Sugar	1g
Protein	20g

TALKING TURKEY

Skinless turkey is a lean meat, containing less than 4 grams of fat per 3-ounce serving. Like chicken, it's high in vitamin B_6, protein, and minerals. Although considered a consummate holiday food, turkey consumption is on the rise in the United States, as companies provide greater diversity of turkey products. Some items, such as turkey bacon and deli meats, are now being offered in low-sodium versions.

Juicy inside with a meaty outer crust, the flavor of these meatballs is heightened with citrus and the heavenly scent of thyme. Serve them over whole-grain noodles. Adapted from EatingWell *magazine.*

¼ cup white whole-wheat flour

1 medium onion, peeled and cut into chunks

3 cloves garlic, peeled

1 tablespoon grated lemon zest

1½ teaspoons dried thyme, divided

1 pound lean ground turkey

¾ cup salt-free bread crumbs

3 tablespoons grated Parmesan cheese

¼ teaspoon ground black pepper

2 teaspoons olive oil

½ cup dry white wine

1¾ cups low-sodium chicken broth

1½ tablespoons lemon juice

1 Place flour in a shallow bowl and set aside. Reserve 1 tablespoon flour.

2 Place onion, garlic, zest, and 1 teaspoon thyme in a food processor and pulse briefly. Transfer mixture to a large bowl and stir in ground turkey, bread crumbs, cheese, and pepper.

3 Pinch off 2 tablespoons at a time and shape into meatballs. Roll the meatballs in the flour to lightly coat. Heat oil in a large skillet over medium heat. Add meatballs and cook until browned, about 5 minutes. Remove meatballs from the skillet and set aside.

4 Add wine to the pan, increase heat to medium-high, and cook, scraping up any browned bits, until almost evaporated, about 1 minute. Add broth and bring to a boil. Reduce heat to low and return meatballs to the skillet with the remaining ½ teaspoon thyme. Cover and cook about 10 minutes.

5 Remove meatballs again and set aside. Bring sauce to a boil over medium-high heat and cook until reduced to about 1 cup, about 5 minutes.

6 Add lemon juice and reserved flour to a small bowl and whisk until smooth. Add flour mixture to sauce and simmer, whisking constantly, until slightly thickened, 1–2 minutes. Remove from heat and return meatballs to the skillet, swirling to coat. Serve immediately.

Ground Turkey Sloppy Joes

Tangy, sweet, and slightly tart, these sloppy joes are every bit as good as the salty ones you used to enjoy.

1 pound lean ground turkey

1 medium onion, peeled and diced

3 cloves garlic, peeled and minced

1 medium red bell pepper, seeded and diced

1 medium tomato, diced

1 (8-ounce) can no-salt-added tomato sauce

1 (6-ounce) can no-salt-added tomato paste

¼ cup apple cider vinegar

2 tablespoons light brown sugar

1 teaspoon dried oregano

½ teaspoon ground cumin

¼ teaspoon ground black pepper

4 Soft and Crusty No-Rise Rolls (see recipe in Chapter 11)

1 Place ground turkey, onion, and garlic in a large skillet over medium heat. Cook, stirring, for 5 minutes.

2 Add bell pepper, tomato, tomato sauce, tomato paste, vinegar, brown sugar, oregano, cumin, and black pepper and stir to combine. Reduce heat to medium-low and simmer for 20 minutes, stirring occasionally. Remove from heat.

3 Divide mixture evenly between rolls. Serve immediately.

SERVES 4	
Per Serving:	
Calories	407
Fat	9g
Sodium	142mg
Carbohydrates	52g
Fiber	6g
Sugar	18g
Protein	30g

CHAPTER 10

Vegan and Vegetarian Dishes

Sesame Tofu with Sautéed Green Beans

SERVES 4

Per Serving:

Calories	238
Fat	12g
Sodium	20mg
Carbohydrates	19g
Fiber	6g
Sugar	6g
Protein	15g

This fantastic vegetarian dish is a great choice for those wanting something meaty. The baked tofu is toothsome and dense, and the sautéed green beans have an irresistible crunch. It's a meal you can sink your teeth into, literally!

1 pound extra-firm tofu

3 teaspoons sesame oil, divided

2 tablespoons toasted sesame seeds

¼ teaspoon ground black pepper

1 medium red onion, peeled and diced

3 cloves garlic, peeled and minced

1 tablespoon minced fresh ginger

1 pound fresh green beans, trimmed and cut into 2" pieces

1 Preheat oven to 425°F. Spray a baking sheet lightly with nonstick cooking spray and set aside.

2 Drain tofu and press gently between paper towels to release excess water.

3 Cut tofu crosswise into 6 equal sections, then turn each section over to lay flat. Slice each section in half lengthwise, leaving 12 (1" × 3½") pieces. Cut each piece in half crosswise; you will now have 24 (1" × 1¾") pieces.

4 Place tofu in a medium bowl, add 2 teaspoons oil, and toss gently to coat. Arrange tofu on the prepared baking sheet and sprinkle evenly with sesame seeds and pepper.

5 Place baking sheet on middle rack of oven and bake for 25–30 minutes, turning tofu once halfway through cooking time.

6 While tofu is baking, heat remaining 1 teaspoon oil in a large skillet over medium heat. Add onion, garlic, and ginger and sauté for 2 minutes.

7 Add green beans and sauté for 5–8 minutes.

8 Remove tofu from the oven and add to the skillet. Stir to coat and serve immediately.

Whole-Grain Penne with Lemony Roasted Asparagus

Such fabulous flavor with so few ingredients! Oven roasting draws out depth in the vegetables, punctuated by the citrus burst.

SERVES 6

Per Serving:

Calories	305
Fat	3g
Sodium	27mg
Carbohydrates	60g
Fiber	12g
Sugar	6g
Protein	14g

ROASTING FOR FLAVOR

Roasting is simply cooking food at a very high temperature. You can roast in an oven, or you can roast over an open flame. Oven roasting allows for convenience and control. You're able to adjust not only the temperature of the oven but the proximity of the food to the flame. The roasting process allows the natural sugars present in many foods to caramelize, leaving the cooked versions much sweeter and more complex than they were when raw.

1½ pounds fresh asparagus, trimmed and cut into 2" pieces
8 ounces button mushrooms, sliced
1 medium red onion, peeled and diced
1 tablespoon olive oil
3 tablespoons lemon juice, divided
¼ teaspoon ground black pepper
1 (16-ounce) package whole-grain penne
1 tablespoon grated lemon zest
2 tablespoons chopped fresh dill

1 Preheat oven to 450°F. Line a large baking sheet with foil and set aside.
2 Place asparagus, mushrooms, and onion in a medium bowl. Add oil, 2 tablespoons lemon juice, and pepper and toss to coat. Spread onto the prepared baking sheet. Place on middle rack in oven and bake for 20 minutes.
3 Meanwhile, cook penne according to package directions, omitting salt. Drain and transfer to a large bowl.
4 Add roasted vegetables to pasta, along with all the cooking juices. Add lemon zest, dill, and remaining 1 tablespoon lemon juice and toss to coat. Serve immediately.

Pesto Rice with Portabella Mushrooms

This one-pot vegetarian meal is perfect for potluck parties. It's best made with white basmati rice, but it's equally delicious with your choice of whole-grain pasta.

2 cups basmati rice

3 cups water

1 tablespoon olive oil

1 medium onion, peeled and chopped

2 cloves garlic, peeled and minced

8 ounces baby bella mushrooms

6 tablespoons Basil Pesto (see recipe in Chapter 4)

¼ teaspoon ground black pepper

1 Measure rice into a fine-mesh sieve and rinse under cold running water. Transfer rice to a medium saucepan and add water. Place pan over medium-high heat and bring to a boil. As soon as water begins to boil, immediately reduce heat to low, cover, and simmer for 15 minutes.

2 Remove pan from heat and fluff rice using a fork. Set aside.

3 Heat oil in a medium skillet over medium heat. Add onion and garlic and cook, stirring, for 2 minutes.

4 Add mushrooms and sauté until tender, about 4 minutes. Remove from heat.

5 Add rice, pesto, and pepper to the pan. Stir to combine. Serve immediately.

SERVES 6

Per Serving:

Calories	291
Fat	9g
Sodium	21mg
Carbohydrates	44g
Fiber	2g
Sugar	1g
Protein	6g

RICE TIP

If you have the time, soak your basmati rice for 30 minutes before cooking. Measure rice into a fine-mesh sieve and rinse repeatedly under cool running water. Place rice into cooking pot, add desired amount of water, and let sit. The soaking water can be used to cook the rice, with no draining necessary. This soaking process will enhance the flavor and texture of the rice.

Spicy Chickpea Tacos with Arugula

A thick and spicy sauce, meaty chickpeas, the peppery cool of arugula, and the crunchy bite of corn taco shells add up to super-tasty tacos!

SERVES 6

Per Serving:

Calories	288
Fat	8g
Sodium	30mg
Carbohydrates	46g
Fiber	9g
Sugar	10g
Protein	10g

1 (5.8-ounce) package low-sodium taco shells

3 cups canned no-salt-added chickpeas, drained and rinsed

4 tablespoons no-salt-added tomato paste

1 (8-ounce) can no-salt-added tomato sauce

1 tablespoon apple cider vinegar

1 tablespoon light brown sugar

2 teaspoons salt-free chili seasoning

1 teaspoon ground mustard

1 teaspoon onion powder

½ teaspoon garlic powder

¼ teaspoon ground black pepper

⅛ teaspoon dried red pepper flakes

6 cups baby arugula

1 Heat taco shells according to package directions.

2 In a medium saucepan, combine chickpeas, tomato paste, tomato sauce, vinegar, brown sugar, chili seasoning, mustard, onion powder, garlic powder, black pepper, and red pepper flakes and stir.

3 Place pan over medium heat and simmer, stirring frequently, for 10 minutes. Remove from heat.

4 Fill warm taco shells with arugula and chickpea mixture. Serve immediately.

Kale-Stuffed Manicotti

Spinach, Swiss chard, or another dark leafy green may be substituted for the kale in this vegan version of the classic Italian dish.

1 (8-ounce) package manicotti

1 medium onion, peeled and chopped

3 cloves garlic, peeled and minced

7 cups chopped kale

1 pound firm tofu, drained

1 teaspoon salt-free Italian seasoning

¼ teaspoon ground black pepper

⅛ teaspoon dried red pepper flakes

3 cups no-salt-added pasta sauce, divided

2 tablespoons nutritional yeast flakes

1 Preheat oven to 400°F.

2 Cook manicotti according to package directions, omitting salt. Drain and set aside.

3 Meanwhile, spray a medium stockpot with nonstick cooking spray and place over medium heat.

4 Add onion and garlic and sauté until soft, about 3 minutes. Add kale and cook, stirring, for 4–5 minutes more.

5 Remove pot from heat and transfer contents to a food processor. Pulse until smooth. Add tofu, Italian seasoning, black pepper, and red pepper flakes and pulse until smooth.

6 Spread a thin layer of sauce into the bottom of a 9" × 13" baking dish. Fill manicotti with kale mixture and arrange in the dish. Pour remaining pasta sauce over manicotti and sprinkle with nutritional yeast.

7 Cover dish with foil, place on middle rack in oven, and bake until hot and bubbly, 20–30 minutes.

8 Remove from oven and serve immediately.

SERVES 6

Per Serving:

Calories	441
Fat	6g
Sodium	51mg
Carbohydrates	77g
Fiber	7g
Sugar	8g
Protein	2g

NUTRITIONAL YEAST FLAKES

Nutritional yeast is a type of inactive yeast with a zingy, cheese-like flavor, making it a great stand-in for Parmesan cheese in low-sodium and vegan diets. The little yellow flakes can be sprinkled on popcorn, pasta, or anything you'd like to perk up. Nutritional yeast contains important vitamins, such as vitamin B_{12}, often found in meat, so it's an especially nutritious supplement for vegetarians and vegans. Nutritional yeast is sold at Whole Foods Market, many natural food stores, and online. Red Star is an excellent brand, as is Bragg.

Quinoa with Mixed Vegetables and Cilantro Peanut Pesto

AN IMPORTANT NOTE ABOUT QUINOA

Quinoa has a bitter-tasting outer coating on its grains that must be removed prior to cooking. Many brands of commercial quinoa remove this prior to packaging, so you can simply measure the quinoa and cook. But if you're not using organic, prewashed quinoa, don't forget to rinse prior to cooking.

Creamy and filling, like a quinoa risotto, this hearty one-dish meal has a fabulous combination of flavors. It's a great choice for parties and other group events.

1 cup quinoa

2 cups water

1 teaspoon olive oil

1 medium red onion, peeled and diced

2 medium carrots, peeled and diced

8 ounces mushrooms, chopped

1 medium red bell pepper, seeded and diced

3 tablespoons Cilantro Peanut Pesto (see recipe in Chapter 4)

2 scallions, sliced

¼ teaspoon ground black pepper

1. Measure quinoa into a small saucepan. Add water and bring to a boil over high heat. Reduce heat to medium-low, cover, and simmer for 15 minutes.
2. Heat oil in a medium skillet over medium heat. Add onion and sauté for 2 minutes.
3. Add carrots, mushrooms, and bell pepper and cook, stirring, for 8 minutes. Remove from heat.
4. Stir in quinoa and pesto. Sprinkle with scallions and black pepper. Serve immediately.

10-Minute Thai Noodles

These spicy noodles will satisfy your hunger for something healthy and filling. Unsalted chunky peanut butter is specified, but feel free to substitute creamy peanut butter and a tablespoon of chopped unsalted peanuts if you prefer.

1 pound angel hair or capellini pasta

3 teaspoons sesame oil, divided

1 small red onion, peeled and diced

4 cloves garlic, peeled and minced

1 tablespoon minced fresh ginger

1 medium red bell pepper, seeded and diced

½ cup low-sodium vegetable broth

2 tablespoons unsalted chunky peanut butter

2 tablespoons lime juice

½ teaspoon dried red pepper flakes

3 scallions, sliced

1 Cook pasta according to package directions, omitting salt. Drain. Add 1 teaspoon oil to cooked pasta and toss to coat. Set aside.

2 Heat remaining 2 teaspoons oil in a large skillet over medium heat. Add onion, garlic, and ginger and sauté for 2 minutes. Add bell pepper and sauté for 3 minutes. Remove from heat.

3 Stir in broth, peanut butter, lime juice, red pepper flakes, and scallions.

4 Add pasta and toss to coat. Serve immediately.

SERVES 6	
Per Serving:	
Calories	377
Fat	6g
Sodium	20mg
Carbohydrates	66g
Fiber	5g
Sugar	5g
Protein	13g

UNSALTED PEANUT BUTTER

Many supermarkets as well as natural food stores, Whole Foods Market, and Trader Joe's sell unsalted peanut butter. Some stores are even installing their own grinding machines, so you can get the freshest, salt-free peanut butter imaginable. If you cannot locate any locally, unsalted peanut butter is sold online. The vast majority of peanuts in the United States are grown using chemical pesticides; purchase organic, unsalted peanut butter whenever possible.

Asparagus, Swiss, and Ricotta Frittata

Frittatas are impressive, yet ridiculously easy to make. Liquid egg replacement is stocked beside the eggs in most supermarkets.

8 stalks fresh asparagus, trimmed and cut into thirds

1 small shallot, peeled and minced

1¼ cups liquid egg replacement (e.g., Egg Beaters)

¼ cup sliced Roasted Red Peppers (see recipe in Chapter 11)

¼ cup shredded Swiss cheese

1 tablespoon nonfat ricotta cheese

¼ teaspoon ground black pepper

SERVES 4	
Per Serving:	
Calories	112
Fat	4g
Sodium	161mg
Carbohydrates	4g
Fiber	1g
Sugar	2g
Protein	13g

1 Move rack to top of the oven and preheat to 450°F.

2 Steam asparagus in a small saucepan over high heat for 5 minutes.

3 Spray a medium ovenproof skillet with nonstick cooking spray. Place over medium heat, add shallot, and sauté for 2 minutes.

4 Add egg replacement to skillet and remove from heat. Top with asparagus, red peppers, and Swiss cheese. Dollop ricotta over the top and season with black pepper.

5 Place the skillet on the top rack in oven and bake for 10 minutes.

6 Remove from oven. Slide a spatula around and under frittata to loosen. Remove and cut into wedges. Serve immediately.

Zucchini Cakes

SERVES 4

Per Serving:

Calories	94
Fat	1g
Sodium	22mg
Carbohydrates	19g
Fiber	2g
Sugar	2g
Protein	4g

HOMEMADE HORSERADISH SAUCE

Combine 2 tablespoons store-bought horse-radish with ¼ cup non-fat sour cream. Add 1–2 tablespoons of chopped fresh herbs, such as dill or chives, a minced clove of garlic, and freshly ground black pepper. Use immediately or cover and refrigerate until ready to serve.

These scrumptious oven-baked patties are a perfect way to use some of your garden surplus. Garnish them with homemade horse-radish sauce or no-salt-added ketchup.

1 medium zucchini, trimmed and shredded

1 small red onion, peeled and minced

1 large egg white

¾ cup salt-free bread crumbs

2 teaspoons salt-free all-purpose seasoning

¼ teaspoon ground black pepper

1 Preheat oven to 400°F. Spray a baking sheet lightly with nonstick cooking spray and set aside.

2 Press zucchini gently between paper towels to release excess liquid.

3 In a large bowl, combine zucchini, onion, egg white, bread crumbs, seasoning, and pepper.

4 Shape mixture into 4 patties and place on the prepared baking sheet.

5 Place baking sheet on middle rack in oven and bake for 10 minutes. Gently flip patties and return to oven to bake for another 10 minutes.

6 Remove from oven and serve immediately.

Amazing Veggie Casserole with Tofu Topping

This recipe makes use of some of the healthiest and least expensive vegetables: carrots, onions, cabbage, and kale. Add a topping of crumbled extra-firm tofu, bread crumbs, and chopped nuts and you've got an irresistible casserole even skeptics will love. Serve it over cooked brown rice. Adapted from Gourmet magazine.

SERVES 8	
Per Serving:	
Calories	238
Fat	9g
Sodium	69mg
Carbohydrates	33g
Fiber	6g
Sugar	6g
Protein	10g

2 teaspoons plus 2 tablespoons olive oil, divided

2 medium onions, peeled and thinly sliced

½ medium head green cabbage, cored and sliced

1 pound kale, trimmed and chopped

3 medium carrots, peeled and sliced into thin sticks

½ cup low-sodium vegetable broth or water

2 tablespoons low-sodium soy sauce

1½ cups salt-free bread crumbs

8 ounces extra-firm tofu, drained

¼ cup chopped walnuts

2 cloves garlic, peeled

2 teaspoons dried basil

1½ teaspoons dried oregano

1 teaspoon ground paprika

1 Preheat oven to 350°F.

2 Heat 2 teaspoons oil in a large skillet over medium heat. Add onions and cook, stirring, for 2 minutes. Add cabbage, kale, carrots, broth, and soy sauce. Cover the skillet and cook, stirring occasionally, for 10 minutes. Transfer contents to a 9" × 13" baking dish and set aside.

3 Place bread crumbs, tofu, walnuts, garlic, remaining 2 tablespoons oil, basil, oregano, and paprika in a food processor and pulse to combine. Sprinkle over vegetables in baking dish.

4 Place dish on middle rack in oven and bake, uncovered, until topping is golden brown and vegetables are heated through, 15–20 minutes.

5 Remove from oven and serve immediately.

Crustless Spinach Pie

SERVES 8

Per Serving:

Calories	83
Fat	3g
Sodium	63mg
Carbohydrates	10g
Fiber	1g
Sugar	1g
Protein	4g

EAT YOUR SPINACH!

Spinach is low in calories, high in fiber and protein, and an excellent source of vitamins A, B_6, C, E, and K. Spinach also contains many important minerals as well as disease-fighting antioxidants. It's easy to grow at home, can be eaten fresh or frozen, raw or cooked, in both savory dishes as well as sweets. Try it in a delicious Green Mango Smoothie (see recipe in Chapter 12).

This deliciously light vegetarian entrée is addictive. Each bite is filled with delicious rice and spinach in a peppery custard, but without the added fat and chore of a crust.

2 teaspoons olive oil

1 medium red onion, peeled and diced

3 cloves garlic, peeled and minced

10 ounces baby spinach

1½ cups cooked rice

½ cup low-fat milk

2 large eggs, beaten

1 tablespoon grated Parmesan cheese

½ teaspoon ground black pepper

1 Preheat oven to 350°F. Spray a pie pan lightly with nonstick cooking spray and set aside.

2 Heat oil in a large skillet over medium heat. Add onion and garlic and sauté for 2 minutes. Add the spinach and continue to cook, stirring, until spinach has wilted fully, 3–5 minutes.

3 Remove from heat and transfer to a medium bowl. Stir in rice, milk, eggs, cheese, and pepper.

4 Pour mixture into the prepared pie pan. Place on middle rack in oven and bake for 25 minutes.

5 Remove from oven and cool 5 minutes before cutting and serving. Serve warm or at room temperature.

Veggie Baked Ziti

Delicious comfort food at its low-sodium best, this version of baked ziti is packed with fresh vegetables. Water-packed mozzarella is often sold in the specialty cheese section of supermarkets. It's softer and much lower in sodium than its dry counterparts. If you can't find it, substitute shredded Swiss cheese instead.

SERVES 6	
Per Serving:	
Calories	384
Fat	8g
Sodium	180mg
Carbohydrates	65g
Fiber	11g
Sugar	10g
Protein	17g

1 pound whole-grain ziti

1 tablespoon olive oil

1 medium onion, peeled and diced

4 cloves garlic, peeled and minced

1 medium bell pepper, seeded and diced

1 medium yellow squash, trimmed and diced

1 medium zucchini, trimmed and diced

1 (15-ounce) can no-salt-added diced tomatoes

2 (8-ounce) cans no-salt-added tomato sauce

2 tablespoons no-salt-added tomato paste

1 teaspoon light brown sugar

1 teaspoon dried basil

½ teaspoon dried marjoram

½ teaspoon dried oregano

½ teaspoon ground black pepper

¼ teaspoon dried savory

¼ teaspoon dried thyme

4 ounces fresh water-packed mozzarella cheese, shredded

2 tablespoons grated Parmesan cheese

1 Preheat oven to 400°F.

2 Cook ziti according to package directions, omitting salt. Drain and return pasta to the pot. Set aside.

3 Meanwhile, heat oil in a large skillet over medium heat. Add onion and garlic and sauté for 2 minutes.

4 Add bell pepper, squash, zucchini, tomatoes with juice, tomato sauce, tomato paste, brown sugar, basil, marjoram, oregano, black pepper, savory, and thyme and cook, stirring, for 10 minutes. Remove from heat.

5 Pour sauce into the pot of pasta. Add mozzarella and Parmesan and stir to combine. Pour mixture into a 9" × 13" baking dish and cover tightly with foil. Place dish on middle rack in oven and bake for 20 minutes.

6 Remove from oven and serve immediately.

Linguine with Plum Tomatoes, Mushrooms, and Tempeh

Pasta is always an easy and filling dinner, especially for vegetarians, and this sauce adds a new dimension to standard low-sodium fare. The slight acidity of the tomatoes provides a wonderful contrast to the nutty, earthy flavors of the mushrooms and tempeh.

SERVES 6

Per Serving:

Calories	358
Fat	8g
Sodium	27mg
Carbohydrates	60g
Fiber	10g
Sugar	5g
Protein	19g

WHAT IS TEMPEH?

Tempeh is a fermented soybean product sold in firm rectangular cakes. It has a rugged texture and nutty flavor that melds well with many types of food. Cut it into cubes and add to pasta sauce, sauté along with vegetables, or marinate in your favorite sauce and bake. Tempeh is stocked in most supermarkets beside the tofu and refrigerated imitation meat products. SoyBoy and Lightlife are two excellent brands. Tempeh is cholesterol-free and a good source of protein, calcium, and iron.

1 pound whole-grain linguine

1 (28-ounce) can no-salt-added plum tomatoes

1 tablespoon olive oil

1 large onion, peeled and diced

8 ounces button mushrooms, sliced

1 (8-ounce) package organic tempeh, diced

3 cloves garlic, peeled and minced

1 teaspoon salt-free Italian seasoning

½ teaspoon ground black pepper

⅛ teaspoon dried red pepper flakes

1   Cook linguine according to package directions, omitting salt. Drain and set aside.

2   Chop tomatoes and set aside with reserved juice from can.

3   Heat oil in a medium skillet over medium heat. Add the onion, mushrooms, tempeh, and garlic and cook, stirring, for 5 minutes.

4   Add tomatoes with juice, Italian seasoning, black pepper, and red pepper flakes. Cook, stirring occasionally, for 10 minutes.

5   Spoon sauce over pasta and serve immediately.

Coconut Cauliflower Curry

The intoxicating array of coconut, garlic, and ginger makes this a heavenly vegetarian meal. If you don't have garam masala, substitute salt-free curry powder instead. Serve the curry with steamed brown or basmati rice.

1 tablespoon canola oil

1 medium onion, peeled and diced

6 cloves garlic, peeled and minced

1 tablespoon minced fresh ginger

1 tablespoon salt-free garam masala

1 teaspoon ground turmeric

2 tablespoons no-salt-added tomato paste

2 cups low-sodium vegetable broth

1 cup light coconut milk

1 medium head cauliflower, cored and cut into florets

3 medium potatoes or sweet potatoes, peeled and diced

2 medium carrots, peeled and sliced

1 (15-ounce) can no-salt-added diced tomatoes

1½ cups fresh or frozen peas

½ teaspoon ground black pepper

¼ cup chopped fresh cilantro

1 Heat oil in a large stockpot over medium heat. Add onion, garlic, and ginger and cook, stirring, for 5 minutes. Add garam masala and turmeric and sauté until fragrant, about 30 seconds to 1 minute.

2 Stir in tomato paste, broth, coconut milk, cauliflower, potatoes, carrots, and tomatoes with juice. Increase heat to medium-high and bring to a boil.

3 Reduce heat to medium-low, cover, and simmer for 20 minutes.

4 Stir in peas and black pepper and cook 2–3 minutes more.

5 Remove from heat and stir in cilantro. Serve immediately.

SERVES 6

Per Serving:

Calories	178
Fat	6g
Sodium	117mg
Carbohydrates	27g
Fiber	7g
Sugar	11g
Protein	5g

WHAT IS GARAM MASALA?

Garam masala is a ground spice blend used extensively in Indian cooking. Although blends may differ, garam masala typically includes cinnamon, cumin, coriander, cloves, ginger, nutmeg, pepper, mace, star anise, and/or bay leaves. Garam masala is potent in terms of fragrance and flavor, but unlike many curry powders does not tend to be fiery hot.

Spicy Red Lentil Dal with Vegetables

SERVES 6	
Per Serving:	
Calories	198
Fat	2g
Sodium	39mg
Carbohydrates	35g
Fiber	10g
Sugar	5g
Protein	11g

This filling main course is a snap to prepare and sings with the mingling flavors of ginger, garlic, and cilantro. If you prefer less spice, simply omit the chili pepper. Be sure to prep all the ingredients beforehand. Serve the dal over rice, sprinkled with additional cilantro, if desired. Adapted from Fine Cooking.

1 medium onion, peeled and diced

4 cloves garlic, peeled and minced

2 tablespoons minced fresh ginger

1 small serrano pepper, seeded and chopped

2 teaspoons canola oil

1½ teaspoons mustard seeds

1 tablespoon salt-free garam masala or curry powder

1½ cups red lentils, rinsed

½ head cauliflower, cored and cut into florets

4 medium carrots, peeled and cut into 1" pieces

2 large potatoes, peeled and cut into 1" chunks

1 teaspoon ground turmeric

6 cups water

¾ cup chopped fresh cilantro

¼ teaspoon ground black pepper

1 Place onion, garlic, ginger, and serrano pepper in a food processor and pulse briefly to chop. Set aside.
2 Heat oil in a medium stockpot over medium heat. Add mustard seeds. When the seeds begin to pop, stir in garam masala, onion mixture, lentils, cauliflower, carrots, potatoes, turmeric, and water.
3 Increase heat to medium-high and bring to a boil. Reduce heat to medium-low, cover, and simmer until vegetables are tender, 20–25 minutes.
4 Stir in cilantro and black pepper. Serve immediately.

Black Bean Burgers

Garnish this hearty southwestern-flavored veggie burger with homemade guacamole and salsa.

2 (15-ounce) cans no-salt-added black beans, drained and rinsed

1 small shallot, peeled and minced

3 cloves garlic, peeled and minced

1 medium red bell pepper, seeded and chopped

¼ cup chopped fresh cilantro

1 tablespoon lime juice

2 teaspoons salt-free chili seasoning

¼ teaspoon ground black pepper

½ cup salt-free bread crumbs

SERVES 4	
Per Serving (1 patty):	
Calories	348
Fat	1g
Sodium	11mg
Carbohydrates	69g
Fiber	13g
Sugar	3g
Protein	19g

1 Preheat oven to 425°F. Spray a baking sheet lightly with nonstick cooking spray and set aside.

2 Place beans in a food processor and purée until smooth.

3 Transfer beans to a large bowl, add the remaining ingredients, and mix together. Form into 4 large patties.

4 Place patties on the prepared baking sheet. Place baking sheet on middle rack in oven and bake for 10 minutes. Remove from oven, gently flip, and return patties to oven. Bake for another 5 minutes.

5 Remove from oven and serve immediately.

Sweet Potato and Black Bean Burritos

This quick meal goes from stovetop to table in 30 minutes. The filling is an irresistible combination of flavors and textures, both sweet and savory. Spoon it into low-sodium taco shells if you can't find lavash. Adapted from Simply in Season.

1 tablespoon canola oil

3 medium sweet potatoes, peeled and cut into ½" cubes

1 medium onion, peeled and diced

¾ cup unsweetened apple juice, divided

1 (15-ounce) can no-salt-added black beans, drained and rinsed

1 teaspoon ground cumin

½ teaspoon ground cinnamon

½ teaspoon salt-free chili seasoning

¼ teaspoon ground black pepper

4 Garden City All Natural Lavash Whole Wheat Roll-Ups

¼ cup low-sodium salsa

¼ cup nonfat sour cream

¼ cup chopped fresh cilantro

1 Heat oil in a large skillet over medium heat. Add sweet potatoes, onion, and ½ cup apple juice to the skillet and stir to combine. Cover the skillet and cook, stirring frequently, until sweet potatoes are tender, about 20 minutes.

2 Uncover the skillet and add beans, the remaining ¼ cup apple juice, cumin, cinnamon, chili seasoning, and pepper and stir to combine. Cook, stirring, for 5 minutes. Remove skillet from heat.

3 Place lavash on a clean surface. Top each with sweet potato mixture, salsa, sour cream, and cilantro.

4 Fold ends toward the center, then roll from the other side up into a cylinder. Slice burritos in half using a sharp knife. Serve immediately.

Spinach Burgers

These burgers are thick, meaty, and completely vegetarian. The shredded Swiss cheese adds a melty tang while keeping the sodium low. Cooked quinoa may be substituted for the bread crumbs to make delicious gluten-free burgers.

SERVES 4

Per Serving:

Calories	111
Fat	3g
Sodium	66mg
Carbohydrates	15g
Fiber	2g
Sugar	1g
Protein	6g

1 teaspoon olive oil

1 medium red onion, peeled and diced

4 cloves garlic, peeled and minced

1 medium red bell pepper, seeded and diced

6 cups baby spinach

1½ teaspoons salt-free Italian seasoning

½ teaspoon ground black pepper

1 large egg white

¼ cup shredded Swiss cheese

½ cup salt-free bread crumbs

1. Preheat oven to 425°F. Spray a baking sheet lightly with nonstick cooking spray and set aside.
2. Heat oil in a large skillet over medium heat. Add onion and garlic and sauté for 2 minutes. Add bell pepper and sauté for 2 minutes. Add spinach and sauté until wilted, about 2 minutes more. Remove skillet from heat.
3. Add Italian seasoning and black pepper and stir, scraping up the brown bits from the bottom of the skillet. Set aside to cool for 5 minutes.
4. Add egg white, cheese, and bread crumbs to skillet and stir to combine. Form mixture into 4 patties.
5. Place patties on prepared baking sheet. Place sheet on middle rack in oven and bake for 10 minutes. Flip patties and bake for another 5 minutes.
6. Remove from oven and serve immediately.

Tofu Sloppy Joes

If you're skeptical of tofu, give this recipe a try. Freezing and thawing the tofu right in the package changes its texture, giving it a much meatier feel. Add sautéed vegetables, tomato sauce, and a vinegar tang, and it's absolutely transformed. Adapted from The Healthy Cook.

1 (16-ounce) package extra-firm tofu, frozen and thawed

2 teaspoons canola oil

1 medium onion, peeled and diced

1 medium bell pepper, seeded and diced

1 stalk celery, diced

2 (8-ounce) cans no-salt-added tomato sauce

1½ tablespoons apple cider vinegar

1 tablespoon no-salt-added prepared mustard

¾ teaspoon vegan low-sodium Worcestershire sauce

1 teaspoon sugar

¼ teaspoon ground black pepper

4 Soft and Crusty No-Rise Rolls (see recipe in Chapter 11)

1   Drain tofu, wrap in paper towels, and press firmly between two plates to release any additional liquid. Pat dry, then crumble tofu coarsely with a fork or your fingers.

2   Heat oil in a large skillet over medium heat. Add tofu, onion, bell pepper, and celery and sauté for 8 minutes.

3   Stir in tomato sauce, vinegar, mustard, Worcestershire sauce, sugar, and black pepper. Cook, stirring frequently, for 5 minutes.

4   Remove from heat. Divide the mixture evenly between rolls and serve immediately.

SERVES 4	
Per Serving:	
Calories	348
Fat	1g
Sodium	46mg
Carbohydrates	45g
Fiber	6g
Sugar	10g
Protein	18g

VERSATILE TOFU

Tofu soaks up flavors like nothing else, and can be added to almost any type of dish, providing added protein, calcium, and iron. Cube a pound of extra-firm tofu, add to assorted vegetables, and roast. Slice into sticks, bake, and toss with a little nutritional yeast. Crumble and add to a vegetable stir-fry with brown rice. Or use instead of chicken in a vegetarian noodle soup.

Falafel with Tzatziki

SERVES 4

Per Serving:

Calories	195
Fat	3g
Sodium	15mg
Carbohydrates	22g
Fiber	8g
Sugar	6g
Protein	11g

These little vegetarian chickpea patties are such a nice change from the everyday, they'll feel like a special treat. Wrap them in low-sodium pita or lavash or enjoy them plain.

5 cloves garlic, peeled

1 (15-ounce) can no-salt-added chickpeas, drained and rinsed

1 small onion, peeled and roughly chopped

¼ cup fresh parsley leaves

2 teaspoons ground cumin

1 teaspoon ground coriander

¼ teaspoon dried red pepper flakes

¼ teaspoon ground black pepper

1 small cucumber

1 tablespoon chopped fresh dill

1 teaspoon lemon juice

¾ cup plain nonfat Greek yogurt

⅛ teaspoon ground white pepper

1 Preheat oven to 400°F. Spray a baking sheet lightly with nonstick cooking spray and set aside.

2 Mince 2 cloves of garlic and set aside. Place the remaining 3 cloves in a food processor. Add chickpeas, onion, parsley, cumin, coriander, red pepper flakes, and black pepper. Pulse until smooth.

3 Spoon the mixture by tablespoonfuls onto the prepared baking sheet. Place sheet on middle rack in oven and bake for 10 minutes. Remove from oven, gently flip falafel patties, and return to bake for another 5–10 minutes.

4 While falafel is baking, peel cucumber. Slice lengthwise and gently scrape out seeds using a spoon. Grate cucumber, then place in a clean towel and squeeze to remove excess liquid.

5 Transfer cucumber to a medium bowl and add minced garlic, dill, lemon juice, yogurt, and white pepper. Stir to combine.

6 Remove falafel from oven and serve immediately with tzatziki.

CHAPTER 11

Side Dishes and Quick Breads

Lemon Parmesan Rice with Fresh Parsley

SERVES 4

Per Serving:

Calories	172
Fat	2g
Sodium	67mg
Carbohydrates	32g
Fiber	1g
Sugar	0g
Protein	6g

This healthy, quick, and easy side has lots of flavor. Vary the fresh herbs to suit your mood; swap the parsley for cilantro, oregano, or basil.

1 cup basmati rice

1½ cups low-sodium chicken or vegetable broth

2 tablespoons grated Parmesan cheese

2 tablespoons chopped fresh parsley

1 tablespoon lemon juice

½ teaspoon grated lemon zest

½ teaspoon ground black pepper

1 Rinse rice in a fine-mesh sieve, then place in a medium saucepan. Add broth and bring to a boil over medium-high heat.

2 Reduce heat to low, cover, and simmer for 15 minutes.

3 Remove pan from heat. Stir in cheese, parsley, lemon juice, lemon zest, and pepper. Serve immediately.

Roasted Root Vegetables with Orange and Thyme

Cut the vegetables into equal-sized pieces to ensure even cooking in this beautiful vegetable medley.

3 medium carrots, peeled and cut into 1" chunks

3 medium parsnips, peeled and cut into 1" chunks

2 medium sweet potatoes, peeled and cut into 1" chunks

3 tablespoons orange juice

1 tablespoon olive oil

1 tablespoon fresh thyme or 1 teaspoon dried thyme

¼ teaspoon ground black pepper

1 Preheat oven to 450°F.
2 Place all ingredients in a large bowl and toss to coat. Turn mixture out onto a large rimmed baking sheet and arrange vegetables in a single layer.
3 Place baking sheet on middle rack in oven and bake for 30 minutes.
4 Remove from oven and serve immediately.

SERVES 6

Per Serving:

Calories	123
Fat	2g
Sodium	43mg
Fiber	5g
Carbohydrates	24g
Sugar	7g
Protein	2g

THYME TIME

Thyme Is an easy-to-grow perennial herb. Its strong, distinct flavor makes it a great choice for many types of roasts, soups, and stews. When using fresh thyme, gently run your fingers along its woody stem, removing the leaves. Leaves may be added whole or chopped. If fresh thyme is not available, dried thyme is a good alternative.

Sweet and Savory Kale with Tomatoes

SERVES 6

Per Serving:

Calories	53
Fat	<1g
Sodium	63mg
Carbohydrates	10g
Fiber	2g
Sugar	1g
Protein	2g

KALE FACTS

Kale is a member of the cabbage family, grows easily in many climates, and freezes well. Once viewed as a decorative garnish, kale is increasingly taking center stage on the dinner plate. Its high levels of antioxidants make it an effective tool in the fight against cancer and cardiovascular disease. Kale contains twice the recommended daily value of vitamin A per serving, making it a valuable aid against degenerative eye diseases.

The combination of subtle sweetness and tang is addictive and so healthy. Use garden-ripe tomatoes when available, no-salt-added canned tomatoes when not. Adapted from www.rawl.net.

1¼ cups low-sodium vegetable broth, divided

1 medium onion, peeled and diced

3 cloves garlic, peeled and minced

2 tablespoons no-salt-added prepared mustard

1 teaspoon sugar

1 tablespoon apple cider vinegar

1 pound chopped kale

1 cup diced tomatoes

¼ teaspoon ground black pepper

1 Place a large stockpot over medium heat. Add ¼ cup broth, onion, and garlic and sauté for 2 minutes.

2 Add mustard, sugar, vinegar, and remaining 1 cup broth and stir to combine. Stir in kale and tomatoes. Cover the pot and cook, stirring occasionally, for 10 minutes, until kale is tender.

3 Remove from heat and season with pepper. Serve immediately.

Roasted Red Peppers

Roasted peppers are beautiful, delicious, and truly easy to prepare. Use them to add color, flavor, and interest to a variety of dishes, from a simple Swiss cheese and roasted chicken sandwich to a vegetarian hummus wrap to a salad of mushroom, onion, and kale.

3 large red bell peppers

1 Preheat oven to 450°F. Spray a baking sheet with nonstick cooking spray and set aside.

2 Halve peppers lengthwise, then remove core and seeds.

3 Place peppers on the prepared baking sheet, cut-side down. Place baking sheet on middle rack in oven and bake 20–25 minutes, until skins are bubbled and beginning to char.

4 Remove baking sheet from oven and place on a wire rack until peppers are cool enough to handle, about 5 minutes. Gently remove skins.

5 Use immediately or store in an airtight container and refrigerate until use. Roasted peppers can be frozen for up to 3 months.

MAKES 1½ CUPS

Per Serving (½ cup):

Calories	50
Fat	0g
Sodium	6mg
Carbohydrates	9g
Fiber	3g
Sugar	6g
Protein	1g

Israeli Couscous with Sautéed Spinach, Bell Pepper, and Onion

With earthy flavors accented with a splash of citrus, this yummy side can be served either warm or cold.

1⅓ cups Israeli couscous

1¾ cups boiling water

1 teaspoon olive oil

3 cloves garlic, peeled and minced

1 medium red onion, peeled and diced

1 medium red bell pepper, seeded and diced

6 cups baby spinach

¼ cup low-sodium chicken or vegetable broth

2 tablespoons lemon juice

¼ teaspoon ground black pepper

1 Measure couscous into a small saucepan and add boiling water. Place pan over high heat and bring to a boil. Reduce heat to medium-low, cover, and simmer for 12 minutes. Drain excess water.

2 Heat oil in a large skillet over medium heat. Add garlic and onion and sauté for 2 minutes. Add bell pepper and sauté for 4 minutes. Add spinach and sauté until wilted, 3–5 minutes. Remove skillet from heat.

3 Add broth and stir to release the brown bits from the bottom of the skillet. Stir in couscous, lemon juice, and black pepper. Serve immediately.

SERVES 6

Per Serving:

Calories	141
Fat	1g
Sodium	33mg
Carbohydrates	27g
Fiber	2g
Sugar	1g
Protein	5g

WHAT IS ISRAELI COUSCOUS?

Israeli couscous, also known as *ptitim*, is a type of small, round pasta made from wheat flour. It's similar to standard couscous, but much larger in diameter. Israeli couscous cooks quickly and is very versatile, making it a great alternative to rice and other grains. It's sold in supermarkets and specialty food stores in both white and whole-wheat varieties.

Sautéed Spinach with Shallots and Garlic

SERVES 2

Per Serving:

Calories	52
Fat	2g
Sodium	72mg
Carbohydrates	6g
Fiber	2g
Sugar	0g
Protein	3g

Baby spinach requires nothing more than a good rinsing. When using larger spinach leaves, wash well, remove tough stems, then chop coarsely.

1 teaspoon olive oil

1 large shallot, peeled and minced

2 cloves garlic, peeled and minced

6 cups fresh spinach, trimmed

¼ teaspoon ground black pepper

1 Heat oil in a large skillet over medium heat. Add shallot and garlic and sauté for 2 minutes.

2 Add spinach and sauté just until wilted, 3–5 minutes. Remove from heat.

3 Season with pepper and serve immediately.

Roasted Potatoes and Broccoli

The combination of crisp, flaky potatoes and slightly smoky broccoli is so simple and so good. Peel and cube the broccoli stem and add it along with the florets for more fiber and nutrients.

1 medium head broccoli

4 medium potatoes, peeled and cubed

1 medium onion, peeled and cut into wedges

1 tablespoon olive oil

1 teaspoon salt-free all-purpose seasoning

½ teaspoon garlic powder

½ teaspoon ground rosemary

¼ teaspoon ground black pepper

SERVES 6	
Per Serving:	
Calories	153
Fat	2g
Sodium	48mg
Carbohydrates	30g
Fiber	5g
Sugar	3g
Protein	4g

1 Preheat oven to 425°F.
2 Cut broccoli into florets and peel and cube the stalk. Place in a large bowl. Add the remaining ingredients and toss to coat.
3 Spread mixture in a single layer on a large baking sheet.
4 Place pan on middle rack in oven and bake for 30 minutes. Remove from oven and serve immediately.

Roasted Radishes and Brussels Sprouts

RADISH FACTS

Radishes, like carrots, are root vegetables. Radishes and radish greens, as their edible leaves are known, have a pungent, peppery taste. This, along with their often vibrant colors, makes them a great choice for accenting salads. Roasting, braising, sautéing, or steaming radishes mellows their flavor significantly. Radishes are high in vitamin C and fiber and low in calories and sodium.

The roasting process mellows the flavor of both vegetables, leaving them tender and caramelized.

½ **pound radishes, halved or quartered**

1 **pound Brussels sprouts, halved**

1 **tablespoon lemon juice**

1½ **teaspoons olive oil**

½ **teaspoon ground black pepper**

1 Preheat oven to 425°F. Spray a baking sheet lightly with nonstick cooking spray and set aside.

2 Place all ingredients in a medium bowl and toss to combine. Pour contents out onto the prepared baking sheet and arrange in a single layer.

3 Place on middle rack in oven and bake 25–30 minutes. Remove from oven and serve immediately.

Carrots with Ginger, Cilantro, and Lime

Lively and flavorful, this carrot dish is a great partner for Indian fare or grilled meat. For more spice, add half a minced jalapeño pepper along with the other seasonings. Adapted from Fresh *magazine.*

1 tablespoon minced fresh ginger

1½ teaspoons mustard seeds

1 teaspoon ground black pepper

½ teaspoon ground coriander

½ teaspoon ground cumin

¼ teaspoon salt-free curry powder

¼ cup water

1 tablespoon canola oil

2 pounds carrots, peeled and cut diagonally into ½" slices

2 tablespoons lime juice

¼ cup chopped fresh cilantro

1 Combine ginger, mustard seeds, pepper, coriander, cumin, and curry powder in a small bowl and set aside.

2 Place a large skillet over medium heat. Add water, oil, and carrots to the skillet and bring to a boil. Cover skillet and cook, shaking occasionally, until carrots are just barely tender, about 7 minutes. Uncover the skillet and continue to cook until carrots begin to sizzle in the oil, about 2 minutes.

3 Add spice mixture and cook, stirring constantly, for 2 minutes. Remove from heat. Add lime juice and cilantro and stir to combine. Serve immediately.

SERVES 6

Per Serving:

Calories	74
Fat	2g
Sodium	117mg
Carbohydrates	12g
Fiber	4g
Sugar	7g
Protein	1g

WHAT ARE MUSTARD SEEDS?

Mustard seeds are the spicy, edible seed of the mustard plant and come in three main types: white, brown, and black. White mustard seeds are the least pungent and are used to make standard yellow mustard, while the slightly spicier brown seeds are used to flavor Dijon mustard. Black seeds, the most pungent in taste, are often reserved for cooking. All mustard seeds contain cancer-fighting and anti-inflammatory compounds. Mustard seeds can be added to food and eaten either whole or ground.

Curried Butternut Squash

SERVES 6

Per Serving:

Calories	75
Fat	4g
Sodium	5mg
Carbohydrates	11g
Fiber	1g
Sugar	2g
Protein	1g

The roasting process brings out the sweetness of the squash, and the curry adds a savory dimension that's out of this world. Adapted from Taste of Home: Dinner on a Dime.

2 tablespoons unsalted butter

1 teaspoon salt-free curry powder

1 medium butternut squash, peeled, seeded, and cut into 1" cubes

1 Preheat oven to 450°F.

2 Place butter in a 9" × 13" baking dish and put in preheated oven. Remove as soon as butter melts. Sprinkle curry powder over butter, then add squash and toss until evenly coated.

3 Place dish on middle rack in oven and roast 20–25 minutes, until squash is tender and very lightly browned. Remove from oven and serve immediately.

Wheat Berry Pilaf with Roasted Vegetables

Chewy, bright, and incredibly flavorful—thanks to the quartet of roasted vegetables—this makes a great potluck dish and may be served either hot or cold.

¾ cup parboiled wheat berries

2 cups water

1 small bulb fennel, trimmed

3 medium carrots, peeled and sliced

1 medium red onion, peeled and diced

8 cloves garlic, peeled and roughly chopped

1 teaspoon olive oil

¼ teaspoon ground cinnamon

¼ teaspoon ground black pepper

1 Preheat oven to 425°F. Lightly spray a baking sheet with nonstick cooking spray and set aside.

2 Place wheat berries and water in a small saucepan and bring to a boil over high heat. Reduce heat to low, cover, and simmer for 15 minutes. Drain excess water and set aside.

3 Dice white bulb and stems of fennel and place in a medium bowl. Coarsely chop green fronds and set aside.

4 Add carrots, onion, and garlic to the bowl with diced fennel. Add oil and toss to coat.

5 Arrange vegetable mixture in a single layer on the prepared baking sheet. Place on middle rack in oven and roast for 15 minutes. Remove from oven.

6 Transfer vegetables to a medium bowl and add wheat berries, fennel fronds, cinnamon, and pepper. Stir to combine.

7 Serve immediately or cover and refrigerate up to 3 days until serving.

SERVES 6

Per Serving:

Calories	211
Fat	2g
Sodium	79mg
Carbohydrates	43g
Fiber	9g
Sugar	3g
Protein	7g

WHAT ARE WHEAT BERRIES?

Wheat berries are individual kernels of wheat with the outer husk removed. They are a whole grain, containing all the beneficial parts of the plant. Wheat berries can be cooked and eaten whole or ground into flour. They're high in fiber and protein, low in fat, and sodium-free. When cooked, they have a chewy texture and a pleasant, slightly nutty flavor. Standard wheat berries take about an hour to cook; look for parboiled wheat berries to speed preparation. Nature's Earthly Choice is an excellent brand.

Baked Spinach and Pea Risotto

There's something magical about the combination of tastes and textures in this risotto. The wine, broth, and cheese lend so much flavor, and the creaminess keeps you coming back for more. If you're concerned about the sodium in the cheese, eliminate it altogether. Adapted from Real Simple.

SERVES 6	
Per Serving:	
Calories	209
Fat	4g
Sodium	110mg
Carbohydrates	32g
Fiber	1g
Sugar	2g
Protein	7g

SODIUM IN FROZEN VEGETABLES

Many frozen vegetables are just that: frozen vegetables. But others contain things you don't want, such as added salt and sauces. Even "plain" vegetables may have been treated in such a way that elevates their sodium content. When selecting frozen vegetables, check nutrition facts carefully to ensure you're buying the vegetables you want, without anything else.

1 tablespoon unsalted butter

1 small shallot, peeled and chopped

¼ teaspoon ground black pepper

½ cup dry white wine

3 cups low-sodium chicken broth

1 cup arborio rice

1 cup frozen peas

2 cups chopped baby spinach

¼ cup grated Parmesan cheese

1 Preheat oven to 425°F.

2 Melt butter in a Dutch oven or similar lidded casserole pan over medium-high heat. Add shallot and black pepper and sauté for 3 minutes. Add wine and cook, stirring, until almost evaporated, 2–3 minutes. Add broth and rice and bring to a boil.

3 Remove from heat, cover the pot and transfer to the middle rack in the oven. Bake for 20 minutes, until rice is tender and creamy.

4 Remove from oven. Add peas, spinach, and Parmesan and stir to combine. Serve immediately.

Whole-Wheat Couscous with Plums, Ginger, and Allspice

SERVES 6	
Per Serving:	
Calories	138
Fat	4g
Sodium	0mg
Carbohydrates	22g
Fiber	2g
Sugar	3g
Protein	4g

An appealing complexity of flavors in a super-simple package, this side dish is terrific served warm or cold.

1½ cups water

1 cup whole-wheat couscous

2 medium plums, peeled, pitted, and diced

3 scallions, sliced

2 teaspoons minced fresh ginger

¼ cup chopped walnuts

¼ teaspoon ground black pepper

¼ teaspoon ground allspice

1 Measure water into a small saucepan and bring to a boil over high heat. Stir in couscous, reduce heat to medium-low, cover, and simmer for 2 minutes.

2 Remove pan from heat, remove lid, and fluff couscous with a fork. Let stand for 5 minutes.

3 Place the remaining ingredients in a medium bowl. Add couscous and toss to combine.

4 Serve immediately or cover and refrigerate until serving.

Garlic Rosemary Mashed Potatoes

Potatoes often fall flat without the boost of salt, but these salt-free mashed potatoes, made without butter and milk, too, may be the best you've ever had.

6 cloves garlic, peeled

2 tablespoons olive oil

¼ cup low-sodium vegetable broth

1 teaspoon unflavored rice wine vinegar

1 teaspoon ground rosemary

½ teaspoon ground white pepper

¼ teaspoon ground mustard

6 cups cubed red potatoes

1 Place garlic, oil, broth, vinegar, rosemary, pepper, and mustard in a food processor and purée until smooth. Set aside.

2 Place potatoes in a large saucepan and add enough water to cover. Place pan over high heat and bring to a boil. Reduce heat to medium-high, cover, and simmer for 15 minutes.

3 Remove from heat and drain. Mash potatoes. Stir in garlic mixture.

4 Serve immediately.

SERVES 6

Per Serving:

Calories	181
Fat	4g
Sodium	13mg
Carbohydrates	32g
Fiber	3g
Sugar	1g
Protein	3g

ROSEMARY FACTS

Rosemary is a perennial herb with a strong taste and fragrance. It grows in sturdy sprigs with leaves reminiscent of soft pine needles. Rosemary can be used either fresh or dried, and is often ground into a fragrant powder for ease in use. It contains iron and several antioxidants believed to ward off neurological disorders such as Alzheimer's and Parkinson's disease.

Sun-Dried Tomato Couscous with Pine Nuts, Garlic, and Basil

SERVES 4

Per Serving:	
Calories	275
Fat	11g
Sodium	282mg
Carbohydrates	37g
Fiber	4g
Sugar	6g
Protein	8g

Sun-dried tomatoes provide an astronomical amount of flavor to this whole-grain couscous dish. Select sun-dried tomatoes packaged without oil.

1 cup chopped sun-dried tomatoes

2 cups boiling water

1 cup whole-grain couscous

2 teaspoons olive oil

4 cloves garlic, peeled and minced

⅓ cup pine nuts

¼ teaspoon ground black pepper

2 tablespoons chopped fresh basil

1. Place sun-dried tomatoes in a small bowl and cover with boiling water. Set aside for 15 minutes.
2. Remove tomatoes and pour soaking liquid into a measuring cup and add enough water to make 2 cups. Set tomatoes aside.
3. Pour liquid into a small saucepan and bring to a boil over high heat. Stir in couscous, reduce heat to medium-low, cover, and simmer for 2 minutes. Remove pan from heat, remove lid, and fluff couscous with a fork. Set aside to cool for 5 minutes.
4. Heat oil in a medium skillet over medium heat. Add tomatoes, garlic, and pine nuts and sauté for 3 minutes. Remove from heat. Add couscous, pepper, and basil and toss to combine. Serve immediately.

Baking Powder Biscuits

These light and flaky biscuits are table ready in 15 minutes, making them a great choice for any meal. Substitute unsalted butter for the shortening if you prefer.

1 cup unbleached all-purpose flour

1 cup white whole-wheat flour

1 tablespoon sugar

4 teaspoons sodium-free baking powder

4 tablespoons nonhydrogenated vegetable shortening

1 large egg white

⅔ cup low-fat milk

1 Preheat oven to 450°F.

2 Place flours, sugar, and baking powder in a large bowl and whisk to combine. Cut shortening into the mixture using your fingers, and work until it resembles coarse crumbs. Add egg white and milk and stir to combine.

3 Turn the dough out onto a lightly floured surface and knead 1 minute. Roll dough to a ¾" thickness and cut into 12 (2") rounds.

4 Place rounds on a large baking sheet. Place baking sheet on middle rack in oven and bake 10 minutes.

5 Remove baking sheet and place biscuits on a wire rack to cool.

MAKES 12

Per Serving (1 biscuit):

Calories	118
Fat	4g
Sodium	13mg
Carbohydrates	16g
Fiber	1g
Sugar	<1g
Protein	3g

NONHYDROGENATED VEGETABLE SHORTENING

Traditional vegetable shortening is made by adding hydrogen to liquid oil. This chemical process produces trans fats, fatty acids linked to coronary heart disease and high cholesterol. Nonhydrogenated vegetable shortening is made naturally from pressed oils that are solid at room temperature. It's trans fat–free as well as cholesterol-free, making it a good alternative to butter when baking. Spectrum Organic All-Vegetable Shortening is sold at Whole Foods Market and online.

Soft and Crusty No-Rise Rolls

MAKES 8

Per Serving (1 roll):

Calories	150
Fat	2g
Sodium	11mg
Carbohydrates	27g
Fiber	2g
Sugar	2g
Protein	8g

SALT-FREE ALL-PURPOSE SEASONING

If there is one seasoning to find on a low-sodium diet, it's this one! Salt-free all-purpose seasoning is a unique blend of herbs, spices, dehydrated vegetables, citrus zest, and sometimes nutritional yeast. Its combination of flavors can replace salt at the table and in recipes, with no additional sodium. Some excellent brands are Benson's Table Tasty Salt Substitute, Olde Thompson Organic No Salt Seasoning, and Frontier Salt-Free Organic All-Purpose Seasoning Blend. Try as many different blends and brands as possible until you find one or more you truly love.

This quick and easy recipe yields eight rolls that are perfect for sandwiches. It's also flexible—cut the dough into twelve smaller pieces and bake them for 12 minutes to make dinner rolls. Or form the dough into a loaf shape and bake it for 30 minutes. Brushing the rolls with beaten egg before baking gives them a gloriously glossy, golden crust.

1 tablespoon dry active yeast

2 teaspoons olive oil

1 tablespoon sugar

1 teaspoon salt-free all-purpose seasoning

1¼ cups warm water

1¼ cups unbleached all-purpose flour

1 cup white whole-wheat flour

1 large egg, beaten

1 Preheat oven to 425°F. Spray a baking sheet lightly with nonstick cooking spray and set aside.

2 Place yeast, oil, sugar, seasoning, and water in a large bowl. Gradually add in both flours, stirring to combine.

3 Once dough comes together, turn out onto a lightly floured surface and knead, adding up to ¼ cup additional flour as necessary. Knead 5 minutes until dough is smooth and elastic.

4 Cut dough into 8 equal portions and form into rolls. Place on prepared baking sheet and brush lightly with beaten egg.

5 Place sheet on middle rack in oven and bake 20 minutes. Remove from oven and serve immediately, or transfer to a wire rack to cool.

Irish Soda Bread

Authentic Irish Soda Bread seems to be a matter of debate. Many American recipes call for eggs, caraway seeds, and raisins and produce loaves much like tea cake. Other recipes add potato flour or rolled oats, yielding the exact opposite—much heartier loaves without a hint of sweetness. This recipe aims for the latter, producing a heavy, salt-free bread with a good crust, lovely toasted with or without butter.

1¼ cups low-fat milk

4 teaspoons distilled white vinegar

2 cups unbleached all-purpose flour

1 cup white whole-wheat flour

2 teaspoons sodium-free baking soda

3 tablespoons sugar

SERVES 12	
Per Serving:	
Calories	133
Fat	<1g
Sodium	12mg
Carbohydrates	27g
Fiber	2g
Sugar	5g
Protein	4g

1 Preheat oven to 400°F. Spray a baking sheet lightly with nonstick cooking spray and set aside.

2 Pour milk and vinegar into a small bowl or measuring cup and set aside 5 minutes.

3 Place both flours, baking soda, and sugar in a large bowl and whisk to combine.

4 Add milk mixture and stir, first using a spoon, then your hands. Gather up the dough into a ball, place on a floured surface, and knead very briefly, just to smooth the dough and to incorporate ingredients fully.

5 Divide dough into 2 equal portions and shape into small round loaves. Place loaves onto the prepared baking sheet and score an "X" on the top of each using a sharp knife. Gently sift a little flour over the top.

6 Place baking sheet on middle rack in oven and bake 30 minutes. Remove from oven and place on a wire rack to cool. Cool fully before slicing and serving.

Perfect Corn Bread

Per Serving:

Calories	103
Fat	4g
Sodium	13mg
Carbohydrates	15g
Fiber	1g
Sugar	5g
Protein	2g

FABULOUS FAT-FREE CORN BREAD!

Make an equally delicious fat-free version of this corn bread by substituting ¼ cup unsweetened applesauce for the canola oil and skim milk for the low-fat milk. Add ½ cup frozen corn to the batter for an added treat.

This foolproof corn bread strikes the ideal balance between sweet and savory. Substitute white whole-wheat flour for all-purpose flour if you prefer.

1 cup cornmeal

¾ cup unbleached all-purpose flour

1 tablespoon sodium-free baking powder

⅓ cup sugar or maple syrup

1 cup low-fat milk

1 large egg white

¼ cup canola oil

1 teaspoon vanilla extract

1 Preheat oven to 425°F. Grease an 8" baking dish and set aside.

2 Place all ingredients in a large bowl and stir to combine. Pour batter into prepared pan. Place pan on middle rack in oven and bake for 20 minutes.

3 Remove from oven and place on a wire rack to cool. Cool briefly before cutting into squares and serving.

Salt-Free Croutons

Here's a tasty way to use leftover low-sodium bread. These delicious croutons will dress up any green salad or enhance even the simplest of soups.

6 cups cubed salt-free bread

2 tablespoons olive oil

1½ tablespoons grated Parmesan cheese

1 teaspoon salt-free Italian seasoning

1 teaspoon garlic powder

1 Preheat oven to 350°F. Take out a baking sheet and set aside.

2 Place all ingredients in a large bowl and toss to coat. Spread bread cubes evenly on baking sheet. Place sheet on middle rack in oven and bake for 10 minutes.

3 Remove from oven and place on a wire rack to cool. Store croutons in an airtight container until ready to serve.

MAKES 4 CUPS

Per Serving (¼ cup):

Calories	52
Fat	2g
Sodium	10mg
Carbohydrates	6g
Fiber	<1g
Sugar	<1g
Protein	1g

CHAPTER 12

Desserts and Drinks

Vegan Chocolate Chip Cookies

Subtly sweet and absolutely delicious, these cookies have a dry crumb that's downright addictive. Pair them with nondairy milk for the full cookie experience. Adapted from Leslie Cerier, the Organic Gourmet.

MAKES 36

Per Serving (1 cookie):

Calories	74
Fat	3g
Sodium	1mg
Carbohydrates	10g
Fiber	0g
Sugar	4g
Protein	1g

1¼ cups unbleached all-purpose flour

¾ cup whole-wheat flour

⅓ cup canola oil

⅓ cup maple syrup

1 tablespoon vanilla extract

¾ cup semisweet chocolate chips

2 tablespoons water

1 Preheat oven to 375°F. Take out two baking sheets and set aside.

2 Place both flours, oil, maple syrup, and vanilla in a large bowl and stir to combine. The mixture will be quite dry and crumbly. Stir in chocolate chips.

3 Add water and stir to incorporate.

4 Scoop the dough ½ tablespoon at a time and shape into cookies. Place cookies on baking sheets and bake on middle rack in oven for 10 minutes.

5 Remove from oven and transfer to a wire rack to cool. Store cookies in an airtight container.

IS CHOCOLATE VEGAN?

Happily, yes. Although some brands of chocolate contain milk derivatives, others do not. When in doubt, check product packaging carefully. Trader Joe's and Whole Foods Market sell store-brand chocolate chips that are 100 percent vegan and tasty. Many health food stores and supermarkets also stock vegan-friendly chocolate morsels and bars. If you can't find them locally, shop online.

Gingersnaps

Fans of classic gingersnaps will love these dark, aromatic cookies with a crisp bite. And they're not just low in sodium; they're low in fat too!

4 tablespoons unsalted butter

½ cup light brown sugar

2 tablespoons molasses

1 large egg white

2½ teaspoons ground ginger

¼ teaspoon ground allspice

1 teaspoon sodium-free baking soda

½ cup unbleached all-purpose flour

½ cup white whole-wheat flour

1 tablespoon demerara sugar

1 Preheat oven to 375°F. Line a large baking sheet with parchment paper and set aside.

2 Beat together butter, sugar, and molasses in a large bowl. Add egg white, ginger, and allspice and mix. Stir in baking soda, then gradually add both flours. Beat until combined, scraping down the sides of the bowl as necessary.

3 Scoop the dough by tablespoonfuls and roll into small balls. Place balls on lined baking sheet and press down using a glass dipped in the demerara sugar.

4 Place baking sheet on middle rack in oven and bake for 10 minutes.

5 Remove from oven and transfer cookies to a wire rack to cool. Store in an airtight container.

MAKES 18

Per Serving (1 cookie):

Calories	81
Fat	2g
Sodium	6mg
Carbohydrates	14g
Fiber	0g
Sugar	8g
Protein	1g

COOKIE BAKING TIP

Never place cookie dough onto a hot baking sheet; cookies will precook before reaching the oven and end up overly dark. For perfect results, use multiple baking sheets. Measure dough onto a cool baking sheet, bake, then remove cookies to a wire rack. Set the hot baking sheet aside to cool, and start afresh with a second baking sheet.

Vegan Lemon Drops

These vegan cookies pack a huge puckery punch, softened by the sweetness of white chocolate chips. For another great taste, swap the lemon juice and zest for lime.

1¼ cups unbleached all-purpose flour

¾ cup white whole-wheat flour

⅓ cup canola oil

⅓ cup maple syrup

3 tablespoons lemon juice

1 tablespoon grated lemon zest

¾ cup vegan white chocolate chips

1 Preheat oven to 375°F. Take out two baking sheets and set aside.

2 Place both flours, oil, maple syrup, lemon juice, and zest in a large bowl and stir to combine. The mixture will be quite dry and crumbly. Stir in white chocolate chips.

3 Scoop the dough ½ tablespoon at a time and shape into cookies. Place cookies on the baking sheets and bake on middle rack in oven for 10 minutes.

4 Remove from oven and transfer to a wire rack to cool. Store cookies in an airtight container.

MAKES 36

Per Serving (1 cookie):

Calories	73
Fat	3g
Sodium	1mg
Carbohydrates	10g
Fiber	0g
Sugar	4g
Protein	1g

VEGAN WHITE CHOCOLATE

Vegan white chocolate chips are sold at some supermarkets, natural food stores, and online. Although they may be more difficult to find, they're worth the effort. In addition to their sweet, creamy taste, some white vegan chips, such as Oppenheimer, aren't just low in sodium; they're also sodium-free!

Carrot Cake Cookies

MAKES 36

Per Serving (1 cookie):

Calories	67
Fat	2g
Sodium	7mg
Carbohydrates	10g
Fiber	0g
Sugar	4g
Protein	1g

ICE CREAM SCOOPS MAKE PERFECT COOKIES!

Instead of fumbling with tablespoons, scoop out cookie dough using a small, retractable ice cream scoop. Ice cream scoops produce uniform, picture-perfect cookies and reduce hassle and mess. Small scoops are sold at kitchenware shops and other stores as well as online.

These soft whole-grain cookies have the taste and texture of carrot cake! To make the oat flour, measure rolled oats into a food processor and pulse until fine.

3 medium carrots, peeled and shredded

1½ cups unbleached all-purpose flour

¾ cup oat flour

¾ cup light brown sugar

1 large egg white

⅓ cup canola oil

1 tablespoon vanilla extract

1 teaspoon sodium-free baking powder

1½ teaspoons ground cinnamon

½ teaspoon ground nutmeg

¼ teaspoon ground ginger

⅛ teaspoon ground cloves

1. Preheat oven to 375°F. Line two large baking sheets with parchment paper and set aside.
2. Place all ingredients in a large bowl and stir to combine. Dough will be quite sticky.
3. Drop by tablespoonfuls onto the prepared baking sheets. Place one sheet on middle rack in oven and bake for 12 minutes.
4. Remove from oven and transfer cookies to a wire rack to cool. Repeat with remaining baking sheet.
5. Store in an airtight container.

Coconut Chocolate Chip Blondies

Use dark, semisweet, or milk chocolate chips in these irresistibly delicious cookie bars. Add chopped almonds, too, if you like some crunch in your blondies.

5 tablespoons unsalted butter, softened

⅔ cup light brown sugar

2 large egg whites

2 teaspoons vanilla extract

½ teaspoon sodium-free baking powder

¾ cup white whole-wheat flour

½ cup unbleached all-purpose flour

¼ cup unsweetened shredded coconut

½ cup chocolate chips

1 Preheat oven to 350°F. Grease and flour an 8" baking dish and set aside.
2 Place butter and brown sugar in a large bowl and beat to combine. Stir in egg whites and vanilla. Add the baking powder and mix.
3 Gradually add in both flours and coconut, then fold in chocolate chips.
4 Transfer batter to the prepared pan and smooth to even. Place on middle rack in oven and bake for 30 minutes.
5 Remove from oven and place pan on a wire rack to cool completely before cutting into 16 squares and serving.

MAKES 16	
Per Serving (1 blondie):	
Calories	150
Fat	7g
Sodium	11mg
Carbohydrates	21g
Fiber	1g
Sugar	13g
Protein	2g

Mango Crumble

SERVES 8

Per Serving:

Calories	190
Fat	5g
Sodium	3mg
Carbohydrates	37g
Fiber	2g
Sugar	23g
Protein	3g

Sink your teeth into tender chunks of mango with a cinnamon-scented crust. For a juicier filling, omit the cornstarch.

2 medium barely ripe mangoes, peeled, pitted, and cut into 1" chunks

2 tablespoons light brown sugar

1 tablespoon cornstarch

1½ teaspoons minced fresh ginger

½ cup unbleached all-purpose flour

½ cup white whole-wheat flour

½ cup granulated sugar

1 teaspoon ground cinnamon

¼ teaspoon ground ginger

3 tablespoons unsalted butter

1 Preheat oven to 350°F.

2 Place mangoes, brown sugar, cornstarch, and minced ginger in a medium bowl and toss to coat. Pour mixture into an 8" square baking dish and spread to even.

3 In another medium bowl, whisk together both flours, granulated sugar, cinnamon, and ginger.

4 Cut butter into small pieces and add to the bowl. Work butter into the mixture using your fingers until it resembles damp sand and sticks together when squeezed. Sprinkle mixture evenly over the fruit.

5 Place pan on middle rack in oven and bake for 25–30 minutes, until tender. Remove from oven and place on a wire rack to cool. Serve warm or cool.

Mini Cornmeal Rhubarb Crisps

With soft, lemon-flavored fruit blanketed beneath a crunchy, sweet cornmeal crust, these little crisps make a sensational spring dessert for company.

3 cups sliced fresh rhubarb

3 tablespoons granulated sugar

2 tablespoons lemon juice

1 tablespoon grated lemon zest

¼ cup cornmeal

3 tablespoons light brown sugar

2 tablespoons old-fashioned rolled oats

2 tablespoons nonhydrogenated vegetable shortening

1 Preheat oven to 375°F.

2 Place rhubarb, granulated sugar, and lemon juice in a large bowl and toss to coat. Divide mixture evenly between four (4") ramekins.

3 Place lemon zest, cornmeal, brown sugar, and oats in a medium bowl and whisk to combine. Add shortening to the bowl and work into the mixture using your fingers. When a sturdy crumb has been achieved, sprinkle mixture over the rhubarb, dividing evenly.

4 Place ramekins on middle rack in oven and bake for 20 minutes.

5 Remove from oven. Set aside to cool for a few minutes. Serve warm.

SERVES 4

Per Serving:

Calories	189
Fat	7g
Sodium	10mg
Carbohydrates	32g
Fiber	2g
Sugar	20g
Protein	2g

RHUBARB FACTS

Rhubarb is an easy-to-grow perennial vegetable with poisonous green leaves and edible pink or red stalks. Rhubarb has a very tart flavor, which is counteracted by the addition of sugar, so it's seen most often in baked goods and desserts. Rhubarb's high acidity may cause a reaction with some metal cookware, so cook or bake rhubarb in stainless steel or nonstick pans whenever possible.

Peach Cobbler

SERVES 8

Per Serving:

Calories	273
Fat	6g
Sodium	15mg
Carbohydrates	50g
Fiber	3g
Sugar	28g
Protein	5g

This updated version of the classic dessert with heart-healthy whole grain and ripe, juicy fruit can be topped with whipped cream or nonfat frozen yogurt.

6 medium peaches, peeled, pitted, and sliced

⅔ cup plus 3 tablespoons sugar, divided

3 tablespoons lemon juice

1¼ cups unbleached all-purpose flour

½ cup white whole-wheat flour

1 teaspoon sodium-free baking powder

4 tablespoons unsalted butter, melted and cooled

1 large egg white

½ cup low-fat milk

1 tablespoon vanilla extract

1. Preheat oven to 400°F.
2. Place peaches, 3 tablespoons sugar, and lemon juice in a medium bowl and toss to coat. Transfer to a 9" × 13" baking dish. Set aside.
3. Place both flours, ⅔ cup sugar, and baking powder in a large bowl and whisk to combine. Add butter, egg white, milk, and vanilla and stir to combine. Batter will be thick. Spoon batter over sliced peaches.
4. Place dish on middle rack in oven and bake for 30 minutes.
5. Remove dish from oven and place on a wire rack to cool. Serve warm or cool.

Guilt-Free Chocolate Cupcakes

MAKES 16

Per Serving (1 cupcake):

Calories	123
Fat	2g
Sodium	4mg
Carbohydrates	25g
Fiber	2g
Sugar	15g
Protein	2g

These vegan, whole-grain cupcakes are low in fat and sodium, so you can indulge in moist, dense, chocolate-laden pleasure with no guilt!

1⅔ cups white whole-wheat flour

¾ cup light brown sugar

¼ cup unsweetened cocoa powder

2 teaspoons sodium-free baking soda

1 cup water

½ cup unsweetened applesauce

1 teaspoon vanilla extract

½ cup semisweet chocolate chips

1   Preheat oven to 350°F. Line sixteen cups in two muffin tins with paper liners and set aside.
2   Place flour, sugar, cocoa, and baking soda in a large bowl and whisk together. Add water, applesauce, and vanilla and stir until combined.
3   Pour batter into the muffin cups, filling roughly ⅔ full. Sprinkle chocolate chips evenly over the batter.
4   Place tins on middle rack in oven and bake for 20 minutes. Remove from oven and place on a wire rack to cool. Cool briefly before serving.

Pound Cake Minis

Save these rich little cakes for a seriously special occasion. Although healthier than classic pound cake, they're still pretty decadent.

½ cup unsalted butter

¼ cup nonhydrogenated vegetable shortening

1 cup sugar

2 large egg whites

2 teaspoons vanilla extract

¼ teaspoon almond extract

½ teaspoon sodium-free baking powder

1¼ cups unbleached all-purpose flour

½ cup low-fat milk

1 Preheat oven to 350°F. Line eighteen muffin cups with paper liners and set aside.
2 Place butter and shortening in a large bowl. Add sugar and beat until fluffy.
3 Beat in the egg whites and extracts. Stir in the baking powder and gradually add in flour, alternating with the milk, and stir until combined.
4 Spoon batter into muffin tins, filling each cup about ⅔ full. Place muffin tins on middle rack in oven and bake for 20 minutes.
5 Remove from oven and transfer to a wire rack to cool.

MAKES 18	
Per Serving (1 mini cake):	
Calories	150
Fat	8g
Sodium	10mg
Carbohydrates	18g
Fiber	0g
Sugar	11g
Protein	1g

Vegan Rice Pudding

SERVES 8

Per Serving:

Calories	148
Fat	2g
Sodium	48mg
Carbohydrates	26g
Fiber	1g
Sugar	10g
Protein	4g

This recipe produces a delicious nondairy rice pudding that's thick and creamy. The pudding thickens significantly as it cools; if you prefer a thinner consistency, stir in a little nondairy milk before serving. Serve sprinkled with ground cinnamon.

1 quart vanilla nondairy milk

1 cup basmati or jasmine rice, rinsed

¼ cup sugar

1 teaspoon vanilla extract

⅛ teaspoon almond extract

½ teaspoon ground cinnamon

⅛ teaspoon ground cardamom

1 Measure all ingredients into a large saucepan and stir to combine. Bring to a boil over medium-high heat.

2 Reduce heat to low and simmer, stirring very frequently, 15–20 minutes.

3 Remove from heat and cool.

Homemade Banana Ice Cream

This dessert contains only one ingredient: ripe (or even overripe) bananas. Yet when frozen and puréed, the crystallized fruit mimics the look, taste, and texture of soft ice cream so perfectly, it's almost magic.

4 large bananas, peeled

1 Place bananas in a zip-top plastic bag and freeze until solid.
2 Remove bananas from freezer and slice into chunks. Place chunks in a blender or food processor and pulse until smooth.
3 Scoop mixture out and serve immediately.

SERVES 4	
Per Serving:	
Calories	105
Fat	0g
Sodium	1mg
Carbohydrates	26g
Fiber	3g
Sugar	14g
Protein	1g

Jumbo Pumpkin Chocolate Chip Muffins

MAKES 6

Per Serving (1 muffin):

Calories	287
Fat	8g
Sodium	20mg
Carbohydrates	51g
Fiber	3g
Sugar	32g
Protein	4g

Moist, dense, and pumpkin-rich, these jumbo muffins are a meal in themselves. Substitute chopped nuts or dried fruit for the chocolate chips if you like.

1 cup pumpkin purée

⅔ cup light brown sugar

1 large egg white

2 tablespoons canola oil

1 teaspoon vanilla extract

1 tablespoon sodium-free baking powder

½ teaspoon ground cinnamon

1 cup white whole-wheat flour

2 tablespoons low-fat milk

⅓ cup semisweet chocolate chips

1 Preheat oven to 400°F. Line a six-cup jumbo muffin tin with paper liners and set aside.

2 Place pumpkin, brown sugar, egg white, oil, and vanilla in a large bowl and stir to combine.

3 Add the remaining ingredients and mix until incorporated.

4 Spoon the batter into the tin, filling each cup about ⅔ full. Place pan on middle rack in oven and bake for 20–25 minutes.

5 Remove from oven and transfer muffins to a wire rack to cool.

Crumb-Topped Mango Muffins

Let these warm, tropical muffins remind you that paradise is just a state of mind. The soft, vanilla-lemon crumb is dotted with juicy chunks of mango, and the tops explode out of the tin with the sweet crunch of macadamia nut crumbs.

¼ cup light brown sugar

¼ cup finely chopped unsalted macadamia nuts

1½ tablespoons plus 1½ cups unbleached all-purpose flour, divided

½ teaspoon ground cinnamon

1 tablespoon unsalted butter

½ cup white whole-wheat flour

1 tablespoon sodium-free baking powder

½ cup granulated sugar

1 large egg white

1 cup low-fat milk

3 tablespoons canola oil

1 teaspoon vanilla extract

1 tablespoon grated lemon zest

1 medium mango, peeled, pitted, and finely diced

MAKES 6	
Per Serving (1 muffin):	
Calories	418
Fat	14g
Sodium	32mg
Carbohydrates	67g
Fiber	3g
Sugar	33g
Protein	7g

1 Preheat oven to 400°F. Spray a six-cup jumbo muffin tin lightly with nonstick cooking spray or line with paper liners. Set aside.

2 Combine brown sugar, nuts, 1½ tablespoons all-purpose flour, and cinnamon in a small bowl. Cut the butter in with your fingertips, processing until it has the consistency of wet sand. Set aside.

3 Place the remaining 1½ cups all-purpose flour, whole-wheat flour, baking powder, and granulated sugar in a large bowl and whisk to combine. Add egg white, milk, oil, vanilla, and lemon zest and stir just until moist. Gently fold in mango.

4 Fill the muffin cups about ¾ full with batter, then top with the crumb mixture, dividing evenly among the cups (about 2 tablespoons each).

5 Place the tin on middle rack in oven and bake for 25–30 minutes. Remove from oven and gently move muffins to a wire rack to cool fully.

Strawberry Shortcake

This is the second-best way to serve gorgeous, ripe, red strawberries—topped only by eating them plain. Add a scoop of nonfat frozen yogurt to make sundaes. Light whipped cream is sold in aerated cans in the refrigerated dairy case of most supermarkets.

4 Baking Powder Biscuits (see recipe in Chapter 11)

1 pound strawberries, stemmed and sliced

2 tablespoons sugar

1 cup light whipped cream

1 Slice biscuits in half. Place the bottom of each in a serving bowl and set the tops aside.

2 Place strawberries in a medium bowl, sprinkle sugar over the top, and stir to coat. Let sit several minutes to release juice.

3 Spoon berry mixture over biscuit bottoms, then cover with tops. Spoon excess syrup over top of biscuits, then garnish with whipped cream. Serve immediately.

SERVES 4	
Per Serving:	
Calories	265
Fat	14g
Sodium	24mg
Carbohydrates	32g
Fiber	3g
Sugar	12g
Protein	4g

Lemon Coconut Scones

SERVES 8

Per Serving:

Calories	255
Fat	8g
Sodium	5mg
Carbohydrates	40g
Fiber	1g
Sugar	17g
Protein	3g

Light and sweet, these lovely, lemon-scented scones are made for a special occasion. Like today!

2 cups unbleached all-purpose flour

⅔ cup sugar

1 tablespoon sodium-free baking powder

5 tablespoons unsalted butter

5 ounces light coconut milk

3 tablespoons lemon juice

1 tablespoon grated lemon zest

1. Preheat oven to 425°F. Line a baking sheet with parchment paper and set aside.
2. Measure flour, sugar, and baking powder into a large bowl and whisk to combine. Cut butter into small pieces and work into the mixture using your fingers. Once the mixture resembles coarse crumbs, stir in coconut milk, lemon juice, and zest.
3. Turn the dough out onto a lightly floured surface and pat into a large 9" round. Using a long, sharp knife, cut the dough into 8 equal wedges. Transfer wedges to the prepared baking sheet.
4. Place sheet on middle rack in oven and bake for 12 minutes. Remove from oven and transfer scones to a wire rack to cool.

Ruby Red Grapefruit Spritzers

An irresistibly rosy hue and mint freshness make these cocktails a satisfying alternative to champagne.

1 teaspoon chopped fresh mint

¾ cup ruby red grapefruit juice

12 ounces unflavored seltzer water

1 Divide mint evenly among four champagne flutes.
2 Add an equal amount of grapefruit juice to each glass, then top with seltzer.
3 Serve immediately.

SERVES 4	
Per Serving:	
Calories	18
Fat	0g
Sodium	0mg
Carbohydrates	4g
Fiber	0g
Sugar	3g
Protein	0g

Green Mango Smoothies

SERVES 4

Per Serving:

Calories	98
Fat	0g
Sodium	20mg
Carbohydrates	20g
Fiber	2g
Sugar	13g
Protein	2g

Tender baby spinach gives these smoothies their bright color and nutrient boost. The sweet and fruity flavor hides the spinach well; close your eyes and you'd never guess it's in there!

1 cup baby spinach
1 medium kiwi fruit, peeled
1 small banana, peeled
1 cup mango juice
½ cup low-fat vanilla yogurt

1 Place spinach in a blender or food processor and purée. Add kiwi and banana and purée again.
2 Add mango juice and yogurt and pulse until smooth and creamy.
3 Serve immediately.

Orange Creamsicle Smoothies

Healthy vegan shakes with a deliciously decadent taste, these Creamsicle smoothies are just like the frozen treats, but better.

1 large navel orange

1 cup vanilla nondairy milk

1 Peel orange, removing as much of the white pith as possible.
2 Segment orange and purée in blender or food processor. Add milk and pulse until smooth.
3 Serve immediately.

SERVES 2	
Per Serving:	
Calories	84
Fat	2g
Sodium	57mg
Carbohydrates	14g
Fiber	2g
Sugar	10g
Protein	3g

Pumpkin Coconut Smoothies

SERVES 3

Per Serving:

Calories	121
Fat	6g
Sodium	36mg
Carbohydrates	10g
Fiber	1g
Sugar	8g
Protein	2g

Thick, creamy, and absolutely delicious, these pumpkin smoothies are a great alternative to the high-fat frozen treats sold each fall.

½ cup pumpkin purée
1 cup light coconut milk
½ cup low-fat vanilla yogurt
1 tablespoon agave nectar

1 Place all ingredients in a blender or food processor and pulse until smooth.
2 Serve immediately.

Maple Mocha Frappé

A creamy concoction of coffee, cocoa, and milk—sweetened with a touch of maple syrup—this frappé is perfect for breakfast or as an anytime pick-me-up.

1 small banana, peeled

½ cup brewed coffee

½ cup low-fat milk

1 cup low-fat yogurt

1 tablespoon unsweetened cocoa powder

2 tablespoons maple syrup

SERVES 4	
Per Serving:	
Calories	103
Fat	1g
Sodium	58mg
Carbohydrates	19g
Fiber	1g
Sugar	15g
Protein	3g

1 Place banana in a blender or food processor and purée. Add the remaining ingredients and pulse until smooth and creamy.

2 Serve immediately.

Piña Colada Smoothies

INGREDIENT TIP

Coconut water is sold in cans and disposable juice boxes, often in the international aisle of grocery stores. Coconut water has the same great flavor of fresh coconut, while being low in fat. Drink cold coconut water as pure refreshment, freeze as ice cubes to subtly flavor cocktails, or add to recipes for a coconut nuance.

In these nonalcoholic coladas, coconut water adds the same great flavor of coconut milk without the fat. Substitute nondairy yogurt for a vegan version.

1¾ cups diced fresh pineapple

1 cup low-fat vanilla yogurt

½ cup coconut water with pulp

1 Place pineapple in food processor and purée.
2 Add the remaining ingredients and pulse until smooth. Serve immediately.

Christy's Cocktails

Slightly syrupy with the pungent taste of anise, Sambuca is an Italian liqueur people seem to either love or hate. Combined with root beer, it's transformed into a delicious cocktail.

2 ounces Sambuca

12 ounces root beer

1   Fill two glasses with ice.
2   Pour 1 ounce Sambuca into each glass.
3   Divide root beer evenly between the two glasses. Serve immediately.

Thin Mint Cocoa

This healthy vegan version of the traditional treat will make mouths and tummies tingle.

3½ cups vanilla nondairy milk

¼ cup unsweetened cocoa powder

¼ cup light brown sugar

¼ teaspoon peppermint extract

1   Measure milk into a medium saucepan and place over medium-high heat. Once milk begins to steam, 3–5 minutes, add cocoa and brown sugar and whisk to combine.
2   Remove from heat. Stir in peppermint extract and serve immediately.

Donno's Mojitos

Fresh and invigorating, these Cuban cocktails will leave you begging for more. A nonalcoholic version, or nojito, can be made without the rum. Many thanks to Donno for the wonderful recipe!

8 fresh mint leaves

2 tablespoons lime juice

2 tablespoons turbinado sugar

2 ounces white rum

12 ounces unflavored seltzer water

2 small lime wedges

1 Divide mint leaves equally between two glasses. Using a wooden spoon, rub the leaves all over the insides of the glasses.

2 Divide lime juice and sugar evenly between the two glasses. Use the spoon to agitate the contents, dissolving the sugar and thoroughly combining the ingredients.

3 Fill both glasses to the top with ice. Divide rum evenly between the two glasses, pouring the rum over the ice.

4 Fill glasses with seltzer and garnish with lime wedges. Serve immediately.

SERVES 2

Per Serving:

Calories	117
Fat	0g
Sodium	36mg
Carbohydrates	14g
Fiber	0g
Sugar	13g
Protein	0g

DIFFERENT TYPES OF SUGAR

Cane sugar comes in many different varieties, the three standard types being white granulated sugar, brown sugar, and powdered or confectioners' sugar. But there are other alternatives. Evaporated cane juice, also called raw or turbinado sugar, is a natural, unrefined product that can be substituted one-for-one for granulated sugar. Demerara sugar is similar to raw sugar, but with a larger, coarser grain. It's often sprinkled on muffins or scones before baking.

STANDARD US/METRIC
MEASUREMENT CONVERSIONS

VOLUME CONVERSIONS

US Volume Measure	Metric Equivalent
⅛ teaspoon	0.5 milliliter
¼ teaspoon	1 milliliter
½ teaspoon	2 milliliters
1 teaspoon	5 milliliters
½ tablespoon	7 milliliters
1 tablespoon (3 teaspoons)	15 milliliters
2 tablespoons (1 fluid ounce)	30 milliliters
¼ cup (4 tablespoons)	60 milliliters
⅓ cup	90 milliliters
½ cup (4 fluid ounces)	125 milliliters
⅔ cup	160 milliliters
¾ cup (6 fluid ounces)	180 milliliters
1 cup (16 tablespoons)	250 milliliters
1 pint (2 cups)	500 milliliters
1 quart (4 cups)	1 liter (about)

WEIGHT CONVERSIONS

US Weight Measure	Metric Equivalent
½ ounce	15 grams
1 ounce	30 grams
2 ounces	60 grams
3 ounces	85 grams
¼ pound (4 ounces)	115 grams
½ pound (8 ounces)	225 grams
¾ pound (12 ounces)	340 grams
1 pound (16 ounces)	454 grams

OVEN TEMPERATURE CONVERSIONS

Degrees Fahrenheit	Degrees Celsius
200 degrees F	95 degrees C
250 degrees F	120 degrees C
275 degrees F	135 degrees C
300 degrees F	150 degrees C
325 degrees F	160 degrees C
350 degrees F	180 degrees C
375 degrees F	190 degrees C
400 degrees F	205 degrees C
425 degrees F	220 degrees C
450 degrees F	230 degrees C

BAKING PAN SIZES

American	Metric
8 × 1½ inch round baking pan	20 × 4 cm cake tin
9 × 1½ inch round baking pan	23 × 3.5 cm cake tin
11 × 7 × 1½ inch baking pan	28 × 18 × 4 cm baking tin
13 × 9 × 2 inch baking pan	30 × 20 × 5 cm baking tin
2 quart rectangular baking dish	30 × 20 × 3 cm baking tin
15 × 10 × 2 inch baking pan	30 × 25 × 2 cm baking tin (Swiss roll tin)
9 inch pie plate	22 × 4 or 23 × 4 cm pie plate
7 or 8 inch springform pan	18 or 20 cm springform or loose bottom cake tin
9 × 5 × 3 inch loaf pan	23 × 13 × 7 cm or 2 lb narrow loaf or pate tin
1½ quart casserole	1.5 liter casserole
2 quart casserole	2 liter casserole

Index

Healthy and Delicious Mediterranean Recipes Everyone at Your Table Will Love!

THE

EVERYTHING®

HEALTHY

MEDITERRANEAN

COOKBOOK

Nourishing, Delicious, & Effortless Meals!

PETER MINAKI

300 FRESH AND SIMPLE RECIPES FOR BETTER LIVING

PICK UP OR DOWNLOAD YOUR COPY TODAY!

adamsmedia

An Imprint of Simon & Schuster
A ViacomCBS COMPANY